A GUIDE TO

Collaboration

FOR

IEP Teams

A GUIDE TO

Collaboration

FOR

IEP Teams

BY

Nicholas R.M. Martin, M.A.
The Center for Accord
Roanoke, Texas

Baltimore • London • Sydney

Paul H. Brookes Publishing Co.
Post Office Box 10624
Baltimore, Maryland 21285-0624

www.brookespublishing.com

Typeset by Barton Matheson Willse & Worthington, Baltimore, Maryland.
Manufactured in the United States of America by
The Maple Press Company, York, Pennsylvania.

Mr. Martin presents seminars on collaboration in the IEP environment
through Paul H. Brookes Publishing Co.'s professional development
program, Brookes On Location. To learn more, please visit
www.brookespublishing.com/onlocation/speakers/martin.htm
or call 1-800-638-3775.

Library of Congress Cataloging-in-Publication Data

Martin, Nicholas, R.M., 1951–
    A guide to collaboration for IEP teams / by Nicholas R.M. Martin.
        p.   cm.
    Includes index.
    ISBN 1-55766-790-X (pbk.)
    1. Individualized education programs—United States.   2. Children with
disabilities—Education—United States.   I. Title.
LC4031.M314 2005
371.9'043—cd22   2004015227

British Library Cataloguing in Publication data are available from the
British Library.

Contents

About the Author

Nicholas R.M. Martin, M.A., is a conflict resolution consultant who lives near Fort Worth, Texas, with his wife, Kathleen, and daughter, Miya. Nick is a graduate of the University of Pennsylvania and the University of Hartford, and his educational background is in clinical psychology. After many years as a juvenile court psychologist, mental health counselor, and dispute mediator, he has come to focus increasingly on team building and conflict prevention. A considerable part of his more recent work has involved skills-based training for those working in special education.

Nick has been authorized to mediate for several court jurisdictions and serves as a contract mediator for the U.S. Postal Service. He has been providing highly acclaimed and practically oriented training for more than 25 years. He has also taught dispute resolution at the graduate level. Nick is the author of *An Operator's Manual for Successful Living* (DeVorss, 1988) and *Strengthening Relationships When Our Children Have Special Needs* (Future Horizons, 2004). He has also published numerous newspaper and journal articles, some of which can be found at his web site, www.4accord.com.

Preface

This book came about through a series of remarkable circumstances—those many and varied coincidences of just being in the right place at the right time, meeting the right people, and getting the right nudges. It happens to all of us, though who can explain it? If I were reading a book like this one, I might be interested in the background, so perhaps I should tell the story in brief.

My educational background is in clinical psychology. I received a master's degree from the University of Hartford in 1975 and went on to practice as a court psychologist in juvenile corrections and later as an outpatient mental health counselor. As time went by, I found myself doing more and more teaching, as a speaker or trainer in a variety of personal growth topics, usually in response to requests from one or another organization in the community. The most popular topics, changing with each decade, seemed to include stress management, meditative techniques, communication skills, coping with burnout, and dealing with difficult people.

In Austin, Texas, in 1995, I fell into an opportunity to take training in dispute mediation, which spoke to me in a big way as a wonderful integration of law and psychology and as a very helpful and much-needed supplement to our judicial system. Over the next few years, I began to focus more and more on conflict resolution as a topic in itself and progressively developed my own little corner of the universe under the banner of "conflict resolution consultant." As such, I have been providing three services: mediation of disputes (usually for the courts or the Postal Service), facilitation of decision-making conferences (usually for small businesses), and training (for corporations, colleges, and government agencies).

When I moved to Lexington, Kentucky, in 2000, I happened to meet a retired school administrator who advised me, based on my career track, to become a trainer for elected school council members. I went through the required training and soon had the opportunity to teach school councils (a grand total of twice). At one of those training sessions, an elementary school principal, knowing of my interest in conflict resolution, asked me, "Can you train my ARC facilitators?" Probably not surprisingly, my first response was, "What's an ARC facilitator?" And so the process leading to this book began.

I came to understand that ARC in Kentucky means *Admissions and Release Committee*. Under federal law, such committees are established in every public school system across the United States and are in place for roughly 12% of all school-age children. Thus, there are vast numbers of people involved in such committees—parents, teachers, school administrators, resource personnel, and often the children themselves. These committees are known by different names in different states, but all can be considered IEP teams, as their primary role is the development of individualized education programs (IEPs) for those children who are designated as having special educational needs. From my earliest investigations, I was consistently hearing that these committees are often hotbeds of conflict. Perhaps, as that principal had suggested, there was a role I could play here.

Before spending too much time or energy, I decided to present a question to Kentucky's State Director of Special Education—to take it to the top and simply ask, "Is there a need for specialized, conflict-related training in the IEP environment, and, if so, is it already being met?" After all, schools have been in business a very long time, and it seemed highly unlikely that I would be the first person to think of offering such training. With a veritable army of staff and services to assist in every conceivable corner of public education, was it realistic to think there would be a great need for little ol' me?

My question was very quickly answered (by e-mail), and to my very pleasant surprise, I was invited to a meeting with the Assistant to the State Director, who asked the leaders of several parent organizations to join us to discuss this question of whether there was a need and whether it was already being addressed. We met in August of 2001, and the results of that rather lively discussion are presented in the Introduction. The consensus was clear and emphatic: Yes, there was indeed such a need, and, no, it was not being addressed. When they heard what I had in mind about developing training to prevent conflict in the IEP environment, in the words of one of the meeting participants, "We jumped on you like a dog on a bone."

Despite their wonderful support of the idea, however, there was not much they could do at the state level. I would have to explore possibilities at the local level. Here I was very fortunate to receive a great deal of interest and assistance from Peggy Blanton, Director of Special Education for the Fayette County Public Schools, in Lexington. I can easily say that without her very active support, this book and the many workshops from which it evolved would not have become a reality.

Peggy rode shotgun in the design of every phase of the training and placed all 60 of her IEP team facilitators and associated staff in the role of my students (like it or not). And so the workshop "Facilitating in the ARC Environment" was born. With each rendition, the workshop was progressively revised, refined, and eventually renamed "Collaboration in the IEP Environment" because it is not just for those who chair IEP committees but for all who participate in them. Expanding on the workshop material, this book was later developed for the purpose of strengthening that training by serving as a reference for workshop participants and as a means of sharing the information on a much wider basis.

It is as a result of the wonderful response I have received from many different directions that this book has come to be in your hands. For the opportunity to be of service in this small but important corner of the universe, I am sincerely grateful. I would like to acknowledge with deep appreciation the assistance of those who have sponsored my workshop and of my many workshop participants—first in Kentucky and then in Texas. Indeed, they are the hidden co-authors of this book; it is they who have taught me so much of what I now share with you. I would also like to acknowledge and thank the outstanding staff of Paul H. Brookes Publishing who have done so much to help bring vision into form. And I would like to dedicate this book to Peggy Blanton, with deep thankfulness for her faith in me and for giving me a chance.

Introduction

The principal met me at the administration office where I signed in and received my visitor's badge. I don't mind saying I was a little nervous, but her welcoming smile helped me feel more at ease. When she said, "So nice to see you again," she sounded sincere, and that helped a lot.

She escorted me to a conference room where several of the school staff were seated around a table—nice chairs, some snacks and drinks set out for anyone who wanted them. I recognized Bobby's homeroom teacher, but the others were new to me. I wondered if they had been talking about him (or about me) before I got there.

The principal invited me to have a seat, and then Mrs. Langley looked at me and began, "Welcome. I'm so glad you could join us today. What if we just go around the table and introduce ourselves, shall we? I'm Margaret Langley, the Special Education Supervisor, and I'll be chairing our meeting today."

The team members gave their names and said how they work with Bobby. Mrs. Langley circulated a paper with the main topics we would be covering today, and began by clarifying what exactly we were meeting for and a little about how these meetings are run. Then she asked Bobby's reading teacher to get us started, and I was shocked. He said, "Well, he shows a real willingness to cooperate when asked to do things. He has a positive attitude toward school and gets along well with the other kids. He shows strength in his ability to stay on task, and he is really good about asking for help when he needs it. He's a great kid, and I enjoy working with him. Wish I had a few more like him."

Wow. I started to wonder, "Am I in the right room?" I thought my kid was having problems and that's why he needed special education. You sure wouldn't think so from the way that meeting started. It was so different from his other school (but I won't go into that).

Welcome to special education in the 21st century. If the foregoing story sounds far-fetched, it isn't. I have seen it more than once in my observations of IEP meetings. It really is possible to have a smooth, harmonious, efficient, and productive conference. It is also possible to cover all required topics in only half an hour or so. Of course, it isn't always so easy, and the ideals are not always met. And when they are not, one can wonder why that is. It is the purpose of this book to present some tools and techniques to enhance the skills of IEP team participants. This may seem straightforward enough, and yet there's more than meets the eye.

DIFFERENCES AMONG SIMILARITIES

In any room full of IEP team members, there will usually be a wide variety of differences. There will be different levels of skills, training, understanding, and experience. There will be different levels of interest, openness, preparedness, and administrative support. There will be different personality styles and different cultural backgrounds. There will be different school and class sizes and student–teacher ratios. The list goes on and on. Thus, to try and write a book to fit each and every reader equally well would surely be an unrealistic goal.

In the pages that follow, I present all that I know—at least all I know that I think may be relevant and, more important, that I think (and sincerely hope) will be helpful. I ask you to bear with me if I cover topics you already fully understand. Other readers may find those topics to be just what they needed. I also ask for a willingness to be open. In every workshop, I have found that different elements speak differently to different participants, and follow-up several months later reveals benefits for one person that may be very different from those of another.

What follows is an overview, evolved from a great many sources—many *different* sources. I accept from the outset that not all points will apply equally to all readers in all settings. I ask only that you consider what may be of value for you—at your school, under your circumstances, with your unique staff, students, and parents. Consider it. Try it out. Keep what you find to be helpful.

HOW ARE TEAMS DOING?

"If it ain't broke, don't fix it," is a very familiar saying, but how do teams know whether it's broke or not, in the sense of whether their IEP meetings are in any need of improvement or attention? On a scale of 1–10, with 10 being perfect, how smooth, efficient, harmonious, and effective are the IEP teams in a particular school, district, region, or state? Is it important to know?

From what I hear, most schools and districts have no mechanism in place by which to assess the level of satisfaction or dissatisfaction in their IEP team environment. That is, most IEP team leaders, and most school and district administrators, have no routine means of establishing whether those participating as IEP team members are basically satisfied or not and what level of conflict, if any, exists within their teams. Yet a variety of indicators suggests that in fact (and generally speaking) *a high level of dissatisfaction* exists in the IEP environment. Without awareness of how their teams are doing, how can anyone be in a position to do something about it before any dissatisfaction reaches destructive and expensive proportions?

Self-Report Inventories

Those teams and administrators that *do* use some kind of feedback mechanism usually rely on written evaluation forms. These forms are either completed by participants at the end of each meeting or completed later and returned by mail. Such evaluation forms have been called *self-report inventories* and are known to have shortcomings.

The routine evaluation completed by members at the end of each meeting appears to be rarely used. When it is used, participants may be in a hurry to complete the meeting and get on to their other responsibilities. If there are dissatisfactions, who will have to deal with them if not the participants themselves? How fully and honestly are they likely to report? Isn't it likely that a slanted and positive picture will be painted so as not to "make waves" and create more time demands for people who are already very busy?

Evaluations done at the end of a meeting are likely to parallel the server at a restaurant, who makes a point to always ask the customer, "Is everything all right so far?" And how does the average person usually answer, unless he or she is *really* unhappy? Isn't the answer usually "Everything's fine," even when it isn't? And why might that be, except that most people don't want to embarrass anyone, they don't want to make waves, and they just want to get on with it because they have other things to do. The point is that routine self-report inventories may be ineffective and even misleading. How many times do people give the "happy diner response" and just say "fine" to the server at a particular restaurant while at the same deciding never to return?

A second common means of assessing IEP team satisfaction is by asking parents to complete an evaluation form and return it by mail. Not surprisingly, two predictable things tend to happen: the reports are remarkably favorable ("Fine, thank you"), and only a small percentage of evaluations are ever returned. The small sampling leaves open the important question of whether the few truly speak for the whole—what about the other 80% or more who *did not* return their forms? And even when many favorable responses are received, other indicators may be painting a different picture entirely.

Three Formal Indicators

Beyond written evaluation forms, there are a number of other indicators of satisfaction in the IEP environment. One very important group of indicators are the statistics assembled at the state level revealing the number of formal interventions being requested by those who are dissatisfied with their IEP team experience. Of course, unhappy participants are likely to express themselves in a variety of informal ways, too, and most teachers and administrators have had their share of angry phone calls and letters, as examples. Yet beyond phone calls and letters or simply going away mad, there are three specific avenues of recourse provided under law. At any time, an unhappy IEP team member can choose to pursue one or more of these, which include

1. **Formal complaint investigations:** Any time that a person believes that a school has violated a provision of the law, that person may (in writing) request an investigation, and the district is then obligated to respond. Because school personnel serve as agents of their respective districts, it is usually the district that is held liable for any errors or omissions.

2. **Dispute mediations:** Under federal law, mediation must be provided as an option for conflict resolution in the IEP environment. Decision making remains with the parties (not the mediator), and the option of a due process hearing or formal investigation remains open if settlement is not reached.

3. **Due process hearings:** Here, alleged violations of law are presented before a designated hearing officer, very much as during a trial in court. States vary in the qualifications required for those serving as hearing officers and in the degree to which officers have authority over parents versus only over the school districts.

With regard to these three formal options, there is wide variation among states in the extent to which records are kept and made publicly available. A little Internet research, however, will confirm the observation that, nationwide, there are many thousands of formal complaints being filed and investigated. An on-line 2003 report by the U.S. General Accounting Office (GAO) reveals that for the years 1996–2000, an estimated 10 state complaints were filed annually per 10,000 students. While this may not seem like a lot, the number becomes more meaningful when multiplied for the roughly 6.5 million children in the United States, ages 3–21, who are receiving special education services. In other words, roughly 6,500 formal complaints are filed nationwide each year.

The GAO also reported that, in addition to formal complaints, thousands of mediations are being conducted each year to settle IEP-related disputes (7 per 10,000 students), and thousands of due process hearings are being requested, increasing from 7,532 in 1996 to 11,068 in 2000. These formal procedures can involve enormous amounts of time, stress, and money for all involved. The GAO estimated that U.S. school districts spent at least $90 million for conflict resolution in the 1999–2000 school year alone! As if this formal activity were not enough, one can only wonder, just as in the restaurant analogy, how many dissatisfied IEP participants are saying "fine, thank you" and simply keeping their feelings to themselves. This last possibility is very much confirmed by discussion with those "in the know"—the leaders of parent organizations.

Feedback from Interviews

As mentioned in the Preface, the training program from which this book arose began with a meeting with representatives of parent support resources (organizations established to provide guidance to parents of children with special educational needs). These representatives were asked whether they saw a need for specialized training in conflict prevention and resolution, and their response was emphatically *yes*. In the course of that 2-hour conference, 12 specific areas of concern were brought into focus, and these 12 no doubt underlie a great many of the disputes that progress into the three formal procedures listed above.

The vast majority of requests for such interventions come from parents against school districts. In theory at least, *any* member of the IEP team could be dissatisfied and could file a request for some form of intervention. In practice, however, it seems that school personnel handle their dissatisfactions in other ways and rarely (if ever) file a formal complaint, request mediation, or request a due process hearing. Instead, school personnel tend to be the *recipients* of such filings and requests. That is, school staff members are in the position of *responding* to such indicators of dissatisfaction rather than being the instigators of them. Does this mean that only the parent members of the team are dissatisfied? Well, from discussions with teachers and other school personnel, I consistently find that dissatisfaction is really very widespread in the IEP environment, far more so than the use of the three formal dispute resolution processes would suggest.

In just a moment, the specific areas of concern so commonly voiced by IEP team parents will be presented, and these are very likely to be the same dissatisfactions that lead to formal procedures if left unchecked. Before examining these common parent concerns, however, let's touch briefly on some of the *other* sources of conflict in the mix—those not specific to the parent members of the team.

SCHOOL STAFF DISSATISFACTION

Teachers

Classroom teachers are universally overworked and underpaid. Rarely do schools have the means by which to fund the ideal vision of education for the students they serve. In fact, they are usually stretched to the maximum. Class sizes are usually far bigger than desired, and teachers are hard-pressed to provide adequate instruction for the roughly 90% of the children in their classrooms who are *not* designated as having special needs. Of course, there are so many variables that it is rarely safe to generalize, and yet many teachers see the obligations of the IEP environment as an added burden, putting additional demands on an already very long list of responsibilities.

Administrators

When federal law first mandated the formation of IEP teams, as one of a broad set of requirements pertaining to children with special educational needs, the government also promised billions of dollars to make it possible for states to meet these added and extensive responsibilities. However, only a small portion of those funds have been delivered, while the financial burden has actually increased. The National Education Association reported that

> Ever since its initial enactment, the federal law has included a commitment to pay 40% of the average per student cost for every special education student. The current average per student cost is $7,552 and the average cost per special education student is an additional $9,369 per student, or $16,921. Yet, in 2003, the federal government is providing local school districts with just under 18% of its commitment rather than the 40% specified by the law, creating a $10.6 billion shortfall for states and local school districts.
>
> —http://www.nea.org/specialed

The implications are that school districts simply don't have all they need to fulfill their many obligations and that it is a constant balancing act to free up the time, funds, staff, and other resources necessary to meet the educational needs of the children entrusted to them.

Much more could be said in this regard, but the purpose is not so much to point fingers as to clarify the many threads in the fabric that can lead to conflict between the many participants at the IEP table. The IEP team is, I believe, a brilliant vision. It can even be considered *visionary*. Yet it is not an easy vision to bring into form—it requires a great deal of skill, dedication, and understanding from all involved. And whenever people are given demands they feel unable to fulfill and when time is so short for so much to be done, stress is likely to follow, and the feelings that accompany it can easily become the seeds of conflict. Some of the IEP-related concerns of school personnel will be presented in upcoming chapters. At this point, let's just begin with an examination of the parent concerns—it is from these that my collaboration and conflict prevention workshop was first developed. Whether these concerns are universally true or only locally true, or whether they are entirely true or only partially true, is not the issue. Instead, the point is that it can benefit school professionals to be aware of what these frequently voiced concerns are and to find ways to ensure that they are not undermining the harmony and effectiveness of their own IEP team meetings.

Frequently Voiced Concerns
relayed by parent group leaders

1. Parents do not always attend IEP meetings and yet have important contributions to make, and they certainly need to know what is being discussed concerning their children. Developing greater parental involvement in meetings, training events, information exchange, and related activities appears to be a nationwide challenge.

2. Each participant at IEP meetings may have differing objectives and constraints—financial, staffing, available resources, time, and so on—yet too often with poor understanding of, and poor communication with, the other participants.

3. Common emotional responses by parents, for whom an IEP meeting may be the first time they hear that their child has special needs (or hear details about the special needs), include shock, grief, fear, anger, mistrust, and guilt. Parents are typi-

cally not aware that these are to be expected, that their emotions will naturally be intense at times, and that there will be ongoing cycles of emotional response. Parents too often feel alone with their feelings, and school staff may be insufficiently aware of or supportive of the parents' emotions. Unless meaningfully addressed, these emotions can easily interfere with productive involvement with the IEP team. Staff attending IEP team meetings would benefit from training in the emotional experience of parents and the grief process.

4. Parents do not always get evaluation reports ahead of time unless they ask for them. If they did receive copies in advance and help in understanding them, it might reduce some of the emotional intensity and conflict at IEP team meetings.

5. The IEP process is often complicated, confusing, and poorly understood by parents, who need help knowing the relevant laws, policies, procedures, rights, and options. Too often, the support and information that is available comes too late in the process, and it would help parents to have more assistance prior to their first IEP meeting, including better communication from school staff and less use of acronyms and unfamiliar terminology.

6. School and district staff attending IEP meetings frequently have other appointments and commitments that preclude their giving adequate time to the team meeting. This can lead parents to feel disrespected and "railroaded" through a process in which they have no power and little to contribute.

7. Meetings are often scheduled at the convenience of school staff rather than parents, which can add to the parents' perception of an inferior status as members of the IEP team.

8. Parents of children with special needs have often had a history of negative feedback from school staff—their child hasn't conformed to what is expected—and this contributes to a climate of negative expectations and mistrust when IEP team meetings occur.

9. Confidentiality of IEP-related matters is often breached by school personnel, especially in smaller communities where team members know one another in a variety of contexts.

10. General classroom teachers often have a limited understanding of the IEP process. They may see a child with special needs as an unwelcome intrusion in the class and may also see participating on the IEP team as a burden adding to their already heavy responsibilities.

11. Parents at IEP team meetings often feel intimidated by the presence of several school personnel (one against many) and give themselves no equal standing as contributors to the child's educational process. Parents typically give their power away to the schools to know how best to meet their children's educational needs. This lack of self-confidence and excessive trust in others limits the potential of the IEP team. As one parent group leader expressed it, "Too many parents have entrusted the education of their children to somebody else."

12. IEP meetings typically lack a clear structure, including such basic formalities as introductions and a set agenda—who are the participants, what are the team's objectives, how will the team meet them, how much time is available, how often will the team meet, and so on. Tangents and digressions are common, as is suddenly running out of time because someone has to leave for another commitment. It is invariably the parents who are at the greatest disadvantage, yet "when elephants fight, it is the grass that gets trampled"—the children are the ones who suffer for any lack of effectiveness of the IEP team.

The greatest single recommendation to come from my discussions with leaders of parent support organizations was *training*. In any of a variety of settings and formats, the need was seen for training of all those participating in the IEP environment—not just school personnel but parents as well. And so this book began.

Part I

Effective Meeting Management

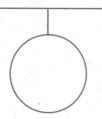

Chapter 1

A Vision of the IEP Team

Under the Individuals with Disabilities Education Act (IDEA) Amendments, whenever a child in a public school is suspected or found to have special educational needs, a team will be formed consisting of the parents and a number of school professionals. Their task will be to evaluate the child's levels of performance, to determine whether a need for specialized educational services exists, and, if so, to design, review, and periodically modify that child's educational program. Clearly it is the intention of the federal government that the education of such children will be not only individualized but also *determined by committee* as a legal obligation.

DESIGNED BY COMMITTEE

If I said I had a dishwasher that you'd think was designed by committee, what would that suggest? If I had a house whose interior decoration looked like it was planned by a committee, what would you expect? It is curious that our culture has come to associate "designed by committee" as if it were an assurance of an inferior product. In fact, the phrase is usually used tongue in cheek in a spirit of humor. Yet under special education laws, schools are *required* to plan for children's educations by committee!

I have no trouble getting a lot of favorable nods when I ask school personnel this question: Wouldn't it be so much quicker and easier if, when a child is found to have special needs, the IEP were designed by a special education teacher, a school administrator, or a director of special education? In other words, wouldn't it be so much easier to skip the committee stage and simply hand an IEP down from above and say, "This is what would be best for this child"? Nearly everyone always says, "Yes!" However, that "yes" is quickly followed by a few qualifiers in the form of "Yes, but . . . ." Let's look at some of those qualifiers now.

If the IEP were handed down from above, it would have several glaring weaknesses, quite apart from violating both the spirit and letter of the law. For one thing, people may not support, and may even resist, those decisions that are handed down to them, as opposed to developed with their own participation and agreement. Except perhaps in the army where it is expected that people will do as they are told without question, most people like to have a say in the decisions that affect them. They want to have what has come to be known as *buy in* or *ownership.* In fact, such inclusion is a founding principle of American society. As early as the 1760s, our founding fathers insisted on being included in the decisions that affected them with such historically significant and familiar slogans as "No taxation without representation." They didn't want the British Parliament to decide what was fair and appropriate to pay. They wanted to be included in the decision-making process—how much tax, from what sources, and for what purposes. Just so, in the present day and age, the federal government has decided that *all* those involved in the special education of children must be represented and have a say in what that education will look like.

A THREEFOLD VISION OF SHARING

The IEP team is thus rooted in a vision that can be viewed as having three fundamental elements of inclusion. That is, the IEP team vision is designed to include those who are affected by having all of them participate in a decision-making process based in *sharing:*

1. **Shared information:** Each member of the IEP team has a unique contribution to make toward a comprehensive understanding of the child's individual needs—classroom observations, home experiences, relationships with peers and siblings, developmental stages, test results, normative information, speech and language development, and so on. Can any one single person know all of this better than the team can, collectively, by sharing?

2. **Shared decision making:** "Two heads are better than one," and the probability of wise decision making becomes so much greater when *many* are involved in the process. By sharing experiences, knowledge, concerns, and resources, the team can be assured of a synergism that is so much less likely when the decisions are made by only one person and handed down to the others.

3. **Shared implementation:** It is the committee members themselves who will act on the decisions made by the group. It is the general classroom teacher who will provide extra support and attention that keeps the child with special needs in the general classroom; it is the special education teacher who will work with the student one-to-one to help meet the goals that the team has set; it is the speech pathologist who will help with the language component, the behavior specialist who will help design a behavior intervention plan, the principal who will coordinate and supervise all staff involved, and the parents who will support the school's efforts in the home. Without that all-important buy in, the different members of the team may not understand and may not support the decisions of the committee—they may even object, resist, and undermine the

decisions. In contrast, when all team members participate, they put their own stamp of approval on a product that will be that much more well-conceived and fully supported. And all three—shared information, shared decision making, and shared implementation—together contribute to the strongest possible plan for the benefit of the child, whose education lies in the hands, minds, and hearts of a committee.

When the committee works together as designed, when it lives up to the vision behind it, the possibility of true synergism emerges. *Synergism* is a wonderful term that warrants a closer look. Merriam-Webster's on-line dictionary defines it as the "interaction of discrete agencies . . . such that the total effect is greater than the sum of individual effects." In simple arithmetic, synergism means that with five people working together, the sum of their combined efforts will be six or even more! Truly, whenever the members of a committee are really working together, they can do so much more than any or all of the individuals by themselves.

Without doubt, the federal government intends for IEP teams to work together and to do so collaboratively rather than adversarially or dictatorially. The school is not a military hierarchy, and education is intended to be a cooperative venture, not authoritative, and to be a partnership between schools and parents for the benefit of the child. This is supported by an Internet visit to the federal Office of Special Education Programs (OSEP):

> Changes in the law represent an effort to ensure that school officials consider parents as decision-making partners in the undertaking of providing special education and related services to their child.
> —http://www.abt.sliidea.org/Reports/FSI_FinalRpt.doc

If the members of an IEP team all do their parts—and do so in the spirit that the legislature intended—they can stand tall and say with great pride, "Yes, indeed, absolutely true: our children's educations were designed by committee!" But how can they get there? How exactly can a particular team manifest this idealistic vision of partner-ship and sharing? This is the subject to which we now turn.

A JOURNEY TOWARD IDEALS

Whenever I ask a group of educators, "Is learning a destination or a journey?" I invariably get a unanimous response. Everyone is quick to agree that it is a journey—that learning is a process that contin-ues throughout our lives. The same is true with regard to learning about the IEP environment and how best to work as teammates in the development of well-designed education programs. Just as any-one on a journey benefits from a clear sense of direction, so do IEP teams benefit from a clear picture of where they hope to go and what constitutes a great team member and a really good team meeting. What exactly defines excellence in the IEP environment? What should teams be looking for and what characterizes the ideal?

Characteristics of the Ideal Member

If you were going to choose someone to join your IEP team, what characteristics would you be looking for? What do you think de-scribes the ideal team member? Those with experience have no trou-ble listing quite a few strengths, skills, and abilities that help make for success in the IEP environment. These include, but certainly would not be limited to, the following:

Characteristics of Ideal IEP Team Members

- Good organizational skills
- People-oriented attitude
- Good communication skills
- Listening skills
- Sense of humor
- Compassion and understanding
- Flexibility
- Realistic expectations
- Acceptance of limitations
- Commitment to coming prepared
- Patience
- Diplomacy
- Time consciousness

(continued)

- Openness to differing views
- Respect for others
- Ability to be firm when necessary
- Leadership abilities
- Understanding of job responsibilities
- Knowledge of laws and policies
- Ability to keep good notes and records

Most readers can probably add to this list based on what they, in their own experience, have found to be important strengths and skills. A few moments' reflection may bring some meaningful answers to the question, "What has been most helpful when shown by other team members or most troubling when missing?" It can be a productive exercise to ask a group of IEP team members to brainstorm answers to these and similar questions, and then to rate themselves (privately) on a scale of 1–10 as to how well they personally are doing with each of the characteristics listed. Such a self-assessment can be helpful in identifying *"growing edges,"* meaning those areas where members are particularly strong, and those where a little extra attention could sharpen their abilities. That term *growing edges* is really a wonderful one and has much to recommend it; without suggesting right or wrong, good or bad, better or worse, it simply reminds us that so long as we are alive, we are always growing. We are always learning, improving, and taking our next steps on the journey forward from wherever we are today.

THREE CLASSIFICATIONS OF ATTRIBUTES

If the list of characteristics of the ideal team member were sorted into categories, there might be three basic classifications. Some have to do with specific job knowledge, some with professionalism in a more general sense, and some with personality traits, totally apart from the work environment. These three classifications of attributes might thus include

- Job knowledge

- Professionalism

- Personality

It isn't difficult to see that, as examples, respect, temper control, and listening skills are personality attributes that will help team members in almost any setting and that, conversely, limitations in any of these areas are likely to result in troubles no matter what the setting. In contrast, sign language skills are job specific and thus more important for the parents and interpreters of a child with a hearing impairment than for the general classroom teacher or the school principal. In terms of the third category, professionalism, is there any business setting in which such traits as being on time, showing appropriate dress and demeanor, and coming prepared would not be important? Those attributes pertaining specifically to job knowledge would be beyond the scope of this book, but it might be worth taking a closer look at the professionalism and personality traits in the other two baskets.

Professionalism

What comes to mind when you think of the term *professionalism?* Wouldn't it include many of the characteristics listed above, such as coming prepared and being time conscious? It would also, of course, include many others, such as staying on task, being realistic, showing appropriate dress and hygiene, and so many more. This issue of professionalism can be taken a step further by asking **why** these traits are important in the IEP environment (or in any business for that matter). Isn't it true that all of these make it easier for people to do their jobs? They each assist the team in fulfilling its purpose and reaching its goals.

"Keep your eye on the prize" is an expression that serves as a reminder to stay focused on what really matters most, and in the IEP environment, only one thing is ultimately important: the best possible educational plan for the child for whom the meeting has been called. When any one member is unprofessional, it costs everyone on the team, and there is something inherently unjust when the whole suffers for the inconsideration of the few. Yet, the flip side is equally true: the whole team *benefits* by the professionalism of its members. And how does that benefit manifest itself, if not in better use of time, more effective working together, and in the end a better IEP for the child?

Personality Traits

The personality basket includes the "warm fuzzies" that help the members feel good about themselves and the team while helping to reduce friction and conflict. Let's look at these attributes more closely.

What is it about listening skills, empathy, understanding, respect, diplomacy, and a sense of humor that makes them important? What difference, if any, do they make, so long as people are doing their jobs? Well, of course they *are* important, and perhaps more so than is always obvious. When people are good listeners, what are they communicating in their silent attention? Perhaps they are showing that they care, that they are open, that they are respectful and interested. Conversely, what do people communicate when they are *not* being good listeners? Perhaps they are showing that they are too busy, that they *don't* care, or that the feelings and opinions of others are not important. It is a safe bet that many formal complaints and due process hearings have grown from the seeds of such perceptions of uncaring and disrespect, even when those perceptions may have had no real basis in fact.

There are so many wonderful quotes that help illustrate the critical importance of listening and its implications. Here are just a few:

It is the province of knowledge to speak, and it is the privilege of wisdom to listen. —Oliver Wendell Holmes

The first duty of love is to listen. —Paul Tillich

The greatest compliment that was ever paid me was when one asked me what I thought, and attended to my answer. —Henry David Thoreau

You cannot truly listen to anyone and do anything else at the same time.
—M. Scott Peck

Whole books have been written on this very important subject, and most people have growing edges when it comes to really good listening skills.

LEARNING FROM GOOD LISTENERS

Think for a moment of people you consider to be great listeners, people you really like to talk to when something is on your mind or weighing on your heart. Who comes to mind? What is it about them that makes them good listeners? What is it like for you to be in the presence of that good listener? Perhaps you feel safe, respected, free to explore your thoughts and feelings without judgment, and so on. People generally like and appreciate those who listen—and feel good just to be around them. It is also worth noting that conflict is very rare between two people who listen well to one another.

Consider the alternative—what comes to mind when we think of people who are *not* good listeners? Most likely it is the flip side of all that has just been described. We don't feel safe, we don't feel respected, we do feel judged, and we often have conflict.

On a scale of 1–10, with 10 being perfect, how would we rate ourselves as listeners? Is listening one of our growing edges? An enlightening exercise can be to ask a few of our closest friends, relatives, or co-workers what scores they would give us if we asked them to rate us, on a scale of 1–10, as to how good we are at listening.

What about empathy, compassion, and understanding? Surely they have much in common with good listening skills. Don't they so often go together? Don't people who listen well also show understanding and compassion? Many readers will have heard the familiar saying, "People don't care how much you know until they know how much you care." Indeed, these and similar people-oriented qualities go a long way to promoting harmony while minimizing conflict, not just in the IEP environment but almost everywhere that people spend time with other people. Having explored what makes for ideal team players, let's look now at what great players can do to make their meetings the best that they can be.

THE IDEAL TEAM MEETING

Much of what is important about ideal meetings can be learned from the simple exercise of asking any group to think of meetings they have attended that they really enjoyed and found worthwhile, whether social, civic, business, religious, or even family meetings. And what was it about those meetings that made them so enjoyable and worthwhile? It usually doesn't take long for the group to come up with a whole list of characteristics of good meetings, and the list usually includes such attributes as the following:

Characteristics of Good Meetings

- The meeting starts and ends on time.
- Everybody knows each other.
- Participants feel safe and respected.
- No single person dominates the meeting.
- People listen, not just talk.
- The meeting has a clear purpose.
- The team makes good use of time.
- There is comfortable seating.
- No one has hidden agendas.
- There are no interruptions.
- Roles are clear.
- People come prepared.
- People leave with a sense of achievement.
- The room temperature is comfortable.
- Snacks and drinks are available.
- The group feels a strong team spirit.
- People are focused and on task.
- People are present in more than just body.

This list is only a start and far from comprehensive. No doubt readers can add more characteristics based on their own individual experience.

What I consistently find—and it is very interesting to watch—is what happens when the question is asked in reverse: "Think of meetings you have attended that you did *not* like and that you did not find enjoyable or worthwhile. What was it about those meetings that made them that way?" What always seems to happen is that the list of negatives is simply the flip side of whatever was mentioned before when meetings were discussed in the positive frame. Thus, the second phase of the brainstorming session usually looks something like this:

Characteristics of Bad Meetings

- The meeting starts late and ends late.
- People don't know each other.
- People do not feel safe or respected.
- One or two people dominate the meeting.
- Nobody really listens.
- The meeting has no clear purpose.
- The team makes poor use of its time.
- The seating is uncomfortable.
- People have hidden agendas.
- The meeting has lots of interruptions.
- Roles are not clear.
- People are unprepared.
- Nothing is accomplished.
- The room is too hot or too cold.
- No snacks or drinks are available.
- A sense of team spirit is missing.
- People are scattered or doing other things.
- People are present only in body.

As before, readers can probably add even more characteristics to the list, and yet most likely they will again be the flip sides of the positive features that were identified before.

This "flip sides" observation is very significant because it is not that there really are two separate and distinct lists: the good and the bad. Instead, there is only *one* list (the good), and without those positive and desirable characteristics present, the perceptions of the people in the meeting are likely to change very quickly from good to bad.

IMPLICATIONS FOR THE IEP ENVIRONMENT

When these simple and almost obvious observations are applied to the IEP environment, it begins to make perfect sense what can be done to maximize the efficiency, productivity, and enjoyability of IEP meetings. It also becomes predictable that when these features are missing, dissatisfaction, inefficiency, and conflict are very likely to follow. In fact, effective meeting management is the first step toward conflict prevention, and very often the seeds of due process hearings and other indicators of conflict are planted in a poorly run meeting. The absence of some of these key features is readily apparent in the concerns that were voiced by parent group leaders and presented in the Introduction. Whether the features were really missing or not, they were *perceived* to be missing, and it is important to understand that it's our perceptions that drive us, even when they aren't really true!

Some of the recommendations made by workshop participants point directly to how teams can apply their insights about meetings in general to improve their IEP meetings. They include the following:

Characteristics of the Ideal IEP Meeting

1. A meeting time and place are selected that are convenient for all participants.

2. Preconferencing occurs with staff and parents to ensure that

   - All necessary participants will attend
   - Participants will, insofar as possible, be able to remain for the entire meeting
   - Participants will come adequately prepared (each participant must decide what will be most relevant from a

great deal of potentially important information, and the meeting can be streamlined by clarifying beforehand what will be most helpful)

3.   Evaluation results are reviewed in advance, assistance is provided if needed to understand the reports, and support is offered when strong emotional impact can be expected.

4.   Child care has been arranged (through prior arrangements at home, or by school staff or volunteers) in those situations where a parent might otherwise have to bring a young child to the meeting.

5.   The meeting facilitator greets the parents on arrival and meets informally with them before the formal meeting begins. (The parents are never put in the position of walking in on a meeting already in progress between school staff.)

6.   A written agenda is visible to all participants (on paper or posted).

7.   All participants are introduced to each other, including their roles as members of the team.

8.   Ground rules are set and agreed (regarding civility, interrupting, leaving the meeting, cell phones, and so on).

9.   Each member is time conscious; the team budgets the available time and respectfully redirects participants who wander.

10.   An atmosphere of mutual respect exists, and all participants share in and contribute to a common purpose.

11.   Breaks are taken as needed.

12.   Round table seating is arranged in a comfortable setting free from noise and distractions.

13.   The meeting has a clear purpose, and roles and responsibilities are clear for tasks occurring before, during, and after the meeting.

14.   The outcome of the meeting is restated at the end for clarity and any necessary correction.

15.   A written "parking lot" is established for questions and issues to be addressed at a later date (rather than letting them get lost).

16. An open-door policy exists for airing and sharing between meetings.

17. The meeting ends on a positive note, and participants are thanked for their time and contributions.

FOUR KEY CHALLENGES AT EVERY MEETING

It may be helpful to think of the group as having four key challenges in their work as a committee at every meeting. The first is *goal achievement*, ensuring that the team accomplishes its goals for the particular IEP meeting. The three remaining challenges all serve to support goal achievement, and they include

- *Budgeting the available time* so as to maintain progress toward goals

- *Defusing the intensity of emotion* which might interfere with goal achievement

- *Safeguarding a collaborative process* by promoting an atmosphere of mutual respect, ensuring a level playing field for all participants, and encouraging consensus-based decision making

On close inspection, it becomes evident that time management, handling emotion, and maintaining collaboration are all means of ensuring goal achievement. However, if the members of a team remain cool, calm, and collected; very streamlined in their use of time; and fully collaborative but do *not* achieve their goals, then they are in no position to rejoice, nor have they fulfilled their legal obligations. All four of these key elements are important, and yet the team must not lose sight of the prize: a well-designed IEP for the child for whom they meet.

Chapter 2

Conducting
the IEP Meeting

C hapter 1 presents a list of characteristics that might be associated with an ideal meeting. This chapter takes the subject a step further and addresses how exactly teams can bring such ideals into form. Ideal meetings are thus considered from the perspectives of developing agendas, introducing participants, setting the stage, and working with some of the challenges that commonly arise at IEP meetings.

WRITTEN AGENDAS

Speaking in generalizations, it seems that written agendas are not often used at IEP meetings. When they *are* used, they may only be visible to the chairperson, who alone has decided what will be on that agenda. Yet what better way could there be for all team members to know the purpose of the meeting and the topics that will be covered? The use of a written agenda is a simple and yet powerful way to address a number of the features defined in the previous chapter as elements of a good meeting, such as having a clear purpose, staying on task, and making good use of time. A written agenda can also go a long way toward addressing the parents' concern (described in the Introduction) that meetings typically lack a clear structure. It is therefore highly recommended that a written agenda be used as a matter of course. It is also important that the agenda be clearly visible to *all* participants, which can be accomplished by simply posting it on a white board or flip chart or by printing it on sheets of paper that are circulated to the team members as a hand-out. The agenda can include

- The major topics to be addressed at the meeting

- The person responsible for leading the group with regard to that topic

- An invitation for all group members to confirm the agenda and thus to have ownership (perhaps by asking, "Does this sound like a good plan for today?")

- An opportunity for any member to add to the agenda so that it is indeed a product of the group, rather than just one or a few members (e.g., "Is there anything that needs to be added to our list?")

There are, of course, a variety of IEP-related meetings, and each will have its own topics. At the same time, because of legal requirements, there is a short list of standard IEP meeting categories, and most of the topics that will be covered are predictable. Thus, the key elements of most IEP meetings are known well in advance and can simply be adjusted as needed when the participants arrive for the actual meeting.

To follow now is a very general overview of these standard IEP meeting categories and their main elements. It should be used only as a rough guide and verified by consulting with the appropriate special education authorities in the team's particular school district.

THE INITIAL REFERRAL

A. Review referral information to see if it is complete.

B. Determine whether there is a need for evaluation.

EVALUATION AND INITIAL IEP

A. Review evaluation results and school records.

B. Determine eligibility for specially designed instruction.

C. Within 30 days of determining eligibility, develop an IEP to include:

1. Child's level of performance, including physical, communication, cognitive, social, and academic levels

2. Annual goals and short-term objectives

3. Special instructional and related services to meet IEP goals

4. How much of school day child will be in general education

5. When special services will start

6. Where IEP provisions will be implemented

7. When and how child's progress will be measured

TRANSITION

A. For toddlers who have been receiving early intervention services (held at least 90 days prior to third birthday)

1. Consider presence of significant learning delays

2. Consider eligibility for preschool

B. For youth ages 12 or over

1. Transition plan must be developed no later than when those youth without disabilities enter high school (usually age 14)

(continued)

2. Include current evaluation, including vocational assessment

3. Cover postschool and long-range outcomes, including

- Adult status: At 18, will the child need limited or full guardianship?
- Work: Job, job training, and military service
- Postsecondary training: College, literacy programs, vocational training
- Home living: Independent, group home, with parents/relatives, residential?
- Community participation: Ability to avail him- or herself of community resources with or without support
- Recreation: With or without support

THE ANNUAL REVIEW

A. Review IEP and records to see if goals have been met.

B. Determine whether child still requires specially designed instruction.

C. Revise IEP, including places where it will be implemented.

D. Consider whether extended services are required to prevent learning regression.

THREE-YEAR REEVALUATION

A. Review test results and re-determine eligibility.

B. Establish levels of functioning and areas of difficulty.

C. Design a current IEP, including places where it will be implemented.

SPECIALLY REQUESTED MEETINGS for the objectives set by the requester; examples might include unforeseen improvements, unexpected difficulties, or any changes of circumstances that might warrant changes to the IEP before a scheduled annual or 3-year review.

Having a written agenda is truly one of the most effective ways of keeping the group focused and on track. It helps all members know where they are and what remains to be completed before the end of the meeting. It also makes it easy to refocus on the issues if the group should ramble or stray. It provides a wonderful way of including the group members in clarifying *their* goals and objectives, budgeting *their* valuable time, and feeling a well-deserved sense of accomplishment at the end of the day.

Forms and Checklists

Some districts have developed standardized meeting checklists and very specific record-keeping forms for their IEP meetings. These can easily become the main bullets of a printed agenda and help ensure that expectations for the meeting are clear and consistent, that participants come prepared, that a high level of focus is kept, and that nothing important is overlooked. Others have shied away from using forms and checklists, seeing such standardization as too.confining and threatening the personalized attention so critical to the IEP process. Standardization and individualization need not, however, be mutually exclusive. Used with the right intention, such forms and checklists can be very helpful in promoting harmony and efficiency. In fact, it was a checklist of strengths, completed by teachers before each IEP meeting, that helped to set a positive tone in the real-life example presented in the Introduction.

A Sample Agenda

Let's assume, by way of illustration, that today's IEP meeting is for the purpose of a routine annual review. A tentative agenda might include the following segments, which could be written and posted before the meeting begins:

Topic	Person leading
Introductions and stage setting	Sue
Classroom observations	Paul
Test results	Maria
Home observations and report	Jane
Is specially designed instruction still required?	team
How have extended school services been working and are they still required?	André
Modifications to Sally's IEP	team

Asking Is Affirming

As mentioned in the previous chapter, group buy in and ownership are of enormous importance. In order for the collaborative vision of the IEP team to be manifested, it is essential that the participants be included in determining the items on the team's agenda. A wonderful expression to consider is *asking is affirming.* Team members communicate so much by way of valuing, inclusion, respect, and caring when they *ask* rather than tell one another how they should spend their time. It may be worth considering once again the deeply meaningful quote of Henry David Thoreau that was presented in the discussion about listening:

The greatest compliment that was ever paid me was when one asked me what I thought, and attended to my answer.

Before closing the agenda-setting stage of the meeting, the chairperson can ask if the group is in agreement with the proposed agenda and whether any members have anything they would like to add to it. Perhaps one member will suggest:

Topic	Person leading
Possibility of transportation assistance	Jane

Authority and Relevance

Sometimes topics will be proposed for the agenda that are not really part of the particular meeting's purpose, not within the decision-making authority of the group, or not really IEP issues. Diplomatically explaining this point and suggesting an alternative is a good way to protect the limited time of the group while at the same time showing respect for the person proposing the topic. For example, "I am very interested in hearing more about that. I'm not sure that this is an IEP issue, though. Could you and I talk about that together after the meeting, and maybe look into who else could help with that question?" This issue of the IEP team's authority and the meeting's purpose must be kept in mind as the agenda is being developed. The details of what is and is not relevant or within the team's authority can vary by state and district policy and can sometimes be hotly debated. Because these issues have substantial legal implications, readers are urged to explore this topic with their own special education administrators.

TAKING A BREAK

If it is obvious that the meeting will be a long one—more than, say, 90 minutes—the group may want to schedule a 5- or 10-minute break at a specific time. This will allow members to answer urgent messages, use the rest room, and such, without having to leave in the middle of the meeting. As an option, the group may want to decide if it would rather *schedule* a break or, instead, just provide a break at any time that a member *requests* one.

If team members leave during the meeting, consider the disadvantages for the others: Those left behind may feel disrespected, and they may be unable to act without the absent party's information or consensus. In addition, the absent member could be missing important information that is brought up when he or she is away from the meeting. The frequency with which team members come and go from meetings is one of the strongest parent complaints, and such activity can certainly undermine the efficiency and harmony of the group. Therefore, providing breaks in a long meeting can go far toward minimizing this potential disruption. Another strategy, of course, is to establish a ground rule that members will not leave except during agreed-upon break times. (More is said about ground rules in a moment.)

As always, asking is affirming, and the chairperson of the meeting can ask the participants how they would like to handle this issue of breaks and leaving the meeting. The words might be something like, "Team, it looks like we will be having a long meeting today— perhaps two hours or more. Would you like to schedule a break, say, around 10 o'clock, or would you rather we just ask for a break if at any time someone feels a need for one? I'd really like to see us avoid leaving during the meeting. How shall we handle this?"

INTRODUCTIONS

What could be more obvious than that participants should be introduced to each other at the beginning of the meeting, if they don't already know each other? Yet a frequent complaint of parents is that they arrive at a meeting to find a room full of people, half of whom they have never met, and far into the meeting, they still don't know who these people are. The parents don't know the people's names, their staff positions, or why they are here making decisions about the child. Obviously there is a simple fix: to take a few moments at the start of each meeting to be sure that introductions are made.

Alternative Introductions

A standard workshop exercise that always stimulates a lot of good discussion involves asking the participants to compare and contrast a series of possible introductory statements. Consider this first example:

Sample Introduction 1

Hi, my name is Jack Smith, and I'd like to welcome all of you to this IEP team meeting. I think our special education teacher has some updates for us. Mrs. Johnson, why don't you go ahead.

How would you critique this introduction? Is it complete? Is it sufficient? What might be missing? Well, yes, the chairperson has introduced himself, but he hasn't told the group what he does, and nobody else at the table has been introduced by name or role. Maybe there is a little more that would be helpful. Here is another possibility:

Sample Introduction 2

Hi, my name is Jack Smith, and I'd like to welcome all of you to this IEP team meeting. Before we begin, let's take a moment to introduce ourselves. I'm the committee chairman, and this is Nancy Adams, the mother of our special needs child. Let's just go around the table and have each of us say who we are and what our roles are as members of the team. [Each member introduces self with name and title.]

Simple, no? Well, everyone has now been introduced, and that *is* important, but are there any possible problems with this introduction? Is anything still missing that may be important? Note that the chairperson has introduced the child's parent, Nancy Adams, while asking everyone else at the table to do their own introductions. Is Mrs. Adams likely to feel singled out? Might she be wondering, "What's the deal here? Don't they think I can even introduce myself?" Or is she perhaps thinking, "Isn't that nice—to make an extra effort to help me feel welcome!" Well, we really don't know whether Mrs. Adams is a little bit shy and might very much appreciate the kind intention shown by the chairperson or whether she will quickly notice how she has been singled out from the group and will very likely feel offended. How can any team be safe with such uncertainties? The answer is simple: *They can ask her!*

Perhaps on the phone prior to the meeting, when greeting her at the school office, or as a private aside just before the meeting begins, the chairperson can say, "Mrs. Adams, I like to start the meetings by being sure we all know each other and what our roles are as members of the committee. Would you rather I introduce you, or would you prefer to introduce yourself? And would you rather be on a first name basis or would you prefer 'Mrs. Adams'?" The chairperson is far less likely to get into trouble this way—by asking.

Notice that there was a curve ball in Sample Introduction 2: The speaker referred to Mrs. Adams as "the mother of our special needs child." However well-intentioned, there is a great risk of stepping on toes by using such phrases as "special needs child" or any terminology that seems to define people by their differences (autistic, deaf, visually impaired, and so on). While some people might never give this a second thought (or even notice), there are others—perhaps a great many—who take offense at being categorized in this way. Far less likely to lead to problems is to *put the child first,* ideally by using his or her name. Instead of "special needs child," the speaker can say "Johnny" and "Johnny's mother." Napoleon is quoted as saying, "If they want peace, nations should avoid the pin-pricks that precede cannon shots." So often people mean well, and yet something is said that starts a negative process in motion. Avoiding such "pin pricks" is what diplomacy is all about. Let's try this again.

Sample Introduction 3

Hi, I'd like to welcome all of you to this IEP team meeting. Before we begin, let's just take a moment to introduce ourselves. As you know, I'm Jack Smith, Assistant Principal here at Happy Lands Elementary School, and I'll be chairing the meeting. Would it be okay if we go around the table and have each of us say who we are and what our roles are as members of the team?

Today we will be doing an annual review of Johnny's IEP, followed by any questions or comments and any recommendations for changes to his IEP. What if we have our special education teacher start?

Notice what is new or different this time. The chairperson is allowing each member to introduce him- or herself and is using questions rather than statements ("Would it be okay if . . . ?"). While it may seem a minor point, this asking rather than telling can greatly assist in communicating respect and in maintaining an atmosphere of collaboration. Notice also that the chairman has added a brief summary of the purpose of the meeting and a few of the key items on the agenda.

So is the introduction now complete? Does it contain all that it should? Well, it may be a very good start, but as noted earlier, a *written* agenda that is visible to all participants is highly recommended. In addition, it is important that participants be invited to add to the agenda, instead of the agenda being something they are only subjected to. These two key elements can be added to the previous sample introduction by including something like the following:

Sample Introduction 3a

I've jotted down some of our key topics for today on the flip chart, so we can see where we are and be sure we cover all the important things. Does this look like a good plan for today? Is there anything that needs to be added to the agenda before we begin?

Of course, not all is fair game here—the team will not include items that are outside its authority or irrelevant to its task. And it may have to prioritize, if necessary, to ensure that the most important items are covered in the time that is available, while carrying over any items that cannot be completed today. (This should rarely be necessary.) Topics of interest that are beyond the authority and purpose of the team will, diplomatically, be covered at another time and setting.

At this point, are the introductions all done and complete? Well, not if the team wants to really cover all bases and guard against future potential problems. Consider the following addition to the last sample introduction:

Sample Introduction 3b

Now just so we know what to expect, let's take a minute to talk about the structure of our meeting. First of all, we know that it's not possible to predict exactly how long an annual review will take, but we know they tend to run about 1–2 hours, sometimes less. It's now 1 o'clock. Are we all free to remain until 3 if necessary? Will anyone have to be leaving before then?

By clarifying the probable time frame at the outset, participants know what to expect, and they can more wisely budget their available time. If any members should have to leave before the end of the meeting, then their reports and comments can be moved ahead so that they are not unduly rushed when their time comes to speak.

Some people might take offense at the very idea that an IEP meeting may have a time frame, so this issue warrants some explanation. Theoretically, an IEP meeting takes whatever time is required to get the job done on behalf of the child. Any person is at least partly right who says, "If it takes all day and night, that's what we'll have to do." At the same time, what are the implications of this unlimited perspective?

If an IEP meeting takes all day and night, what can be safely assumed (considering that there has probably never been an IEP meeting in history that *really* went all day and night)? It probably means that the team has become bogged down in emotions or is spending excessive time on things that are not really necessary for the achievement of its purpose under federal law. The point is just that very often when time is marching on, it is because that time has not been wisely used: A focus has not been held, sidetracks have been taken, or tempers have risen. The team may be spending lots of time but not spending its time *productively*.

It is important to bear in mind that each of the members at the table has his or her own list of other responsibilities, and it is sometimes a real challenge to cover all of these at the same time. As examples, the teachers who have left their classrooms to attend the meeting have had to arrange coverage until they return, usually according to the school's daily schedule of classes. Substitutes will be covering the classes, but those substitutes may have different classes to cover at specific times on the clock. The various resource specialists may have to be at other meetings, perhaps at other schools, by certain times. When parents attend an IEP meeting, they too have taken valuable time from their other commitments, whether at work or at home. School administrators have to be otherwise unavailable while attending and remaining focused on the meeting. In our real-world circumstances, there simply is no such thing as unlimited time. This is all the more reason why IEP teams must carefully budget their time and use what time they have both efficiently and productively.

Yes, an IEP meeting must take whatever time is necessary to ensure that the rights of the child are being protected. There will certainly, therefore, be times when meetings must be extended, when projected time frames turn out to be insufficient, and when reconvening the meeting will be necessary. Teams can, however, minimize such extensions by carefully planning their meetings and by managing them well from start to finish—with respect for all members and their valuable time.

A final aspect of introductory remarks includes the setting of ground rules and provisions for the efficiency and comfort of those attending the meeting. What follows now might be considered a comprehensive statement of introduction:

Sample Introduction 4 (Complete)

[as before] Hi, I'd like to welcome all of you to this IEP team meeting. Before we begin, let's just take a moment to introduce ourselves. As you know, I'm Jack Smith, Assistant Principal here at Happy Lands Elementary School, and I'll be chairing the meeting. Would it be okay if we go around the table and have each of us say who we are and what our roles are as members of the team?

[as before] Today we will be doing an annual review of Johnny's IEP, followed by any questions or comments, and any recommendations for changes to his IEP. I've jotted down some of our key topics for today on the flip chart, so we can see where we are and be sure we cover all the important things. Does this look like a good plan for today? Is there anything that needs to be added to the agenda before we begin?

[as before] Now just so we know what to expect, let's take a minute to talk about the structure of our meeting. First of all, we know that it's not possible to predict exactly how long an annual review will take, but we know they tend to run about 1–2 hours, sometimes less. It's now 1 o'clock. Are we all free to remain until 3 if necessary? Will anyone have to be leaving before then?

[additions] And so we can make the best use of our time, let's talk a little about any ground rules or guidelines we might want to have for this meeting. We know it's a confidential proceeding and anything we talk about in here is protected information. Any questions or comments about that? And we know we are here for Johnny's benefit and to welcome Mrs. Adams to be an active and equal member of this committee. Agreed? So, Mrs. Adams, please feel free to share any thoughts or suggestions you have, and to be as much a part of this group as any of us, okay?

May I also suggest that we do our best to remain focused and efficient in our use of the limited time we have today? Could we please turn off cell phones and beepers? I've asked the receptionist to hold any calls unless really urgent, and I'll hang a "do not disturb" sign on the door. If anyone needs a phone or bathroom break, we will take a short one after about an hour. Could we agree to avoid leaving the room before that break if possible? I've set some snacks and drinks on the table—please don't be bashful—and if it gets too warm or cold for you, please let me know. Does anyone have any other thoughts in terms of guidelines for our meeting?

Please consider the above only as a model to illustrate how the many facets of an introductory statement might be integrated. Consider also how it sounds to include suggested ground rules and to provide for "creature comforts." Both are very important, although the reasons may not be immediately apparent.

Setting ground rules and inviting the group's commitment to them can be extremely helpful in preventing the disruptions that might otherwise occur. For example, if members agree to remain in the room until a scheduled break, this can help to avoid people getting up and walking out, perhaps without even saying why they are leaving or when they will be back. Similarly, agreeing to turn off cell phones (unless in an emergency) has obvious benefits for helping the group remain on task and focused. Of course, *how* a team sets its ground rules is very important: They must be proposed and invited, rather than imposed and demanded. This seemingly subtle distinction can make a very big difference.

Snacks are an important item, too, and for several reasons. Someone rushing to the meeting from a class or from home may not have had a chance to eat yet, and people tend not to think very clearly when they are hungry. A bowl of individually wrapped candies or other simple snack items and a few bottled juices or waters are inexpensive and may be very much appreciated. Providing them may also reduce the number of times that participants feel a need to take a break. In addition, many people feel a sense of warmth and welcome when offered something to eat or drink. It costs very little and yet can be helpful in promoting the kind of positive atmosphere that makes for the best kind of meetings.

On the next page is a checklist that people who are chairing IEP meetings might like to review and consider. As they develop their own words and style, they may find such a checklist helpful in summarizing the key elements that should be included in a comprehensive introduction—one that sets the stage, promotes team spirit, and helps to safeguard against the kinds of problems that might otherwise arise.

MODEL INTRODUCTION CHECKLIST

Welcome and Introductions

- [ ] Name
- [ ] Role as member of the IEP team
- [ ] Introduction of parent member (if parent prefers)

Purpose of this Team Meeting

- [ ] Referral
- [ ] Evaluation and Initial IEP
- [ ] Annual Review
- [ ] Transition
- [ ] Three-Year Review
- [ ] Specially requested
- [ ] Other: _____

Written Agenda (on board, handout, or flip chart)

- [ ] Objectives for this meeting
- [ ] Invite agreement and any additions from participants

Anticipated Duration of Meeting

- [ ] Typical time frame
- [ ] Anyone leaving early?
- [ ] Agreement to remain for the full meeting

Ground Rules and Guidelines

- [ ] Confidentiality parameters (any limitations?)
- [ ] Encourage parent participation
- [ ] Agreement to maintain focus and efficiency
- [ ] Agreement to avoid interruptions (cell phones, sign on door)
- [ ] Agreement to remain as a group (avoid leaving the meeting)

Creature Comforts

- [ ] Snacks and drinks
- [ ] Temperature and ventilation
- [ ] Noise
- [ ] Breaks

ENSURING A SMOOTHLY RUNNING MEETING

While some of the responsibility for managing the IEP meeting rests with the chairperson, it is also true that the chairperson is not the *only* person at the table. Consistent with the vision of decision-making partnership, *all* members of the team are responsible for the efficient, professional, and harmonious conduct of the meeting. It is up to each of them, therefore, to assist one another with goal achievement, as well as budgeting time, managing emotions, and safeguarding a collaborative process. Let's look more closely now at these four elements and then address some of the common scenarios that can threaten the smooth running of a meeting.

As mentioned before, three of the four key elements of effective meeting management really serve to support the one overarching element, which is to achieve the goals of the particular meeting. Using written agendas, introducing the participants, and establishing ground rules are extremely helpful in this regard. Assuming that these fundamental cornerstones *are* now included, we can reference them only briefly as we turn now to some additional means of ensuring smooth and productive meetings.

Budgeting Time

Perhaps the first step in budgeting time more effectively is to simply *recognize the importance* of doing so. It may be helpful to look at this issue from three perspectives: what promotes effective time management, what impairs it, and what can be done to restore it when efficient time management has become lost.

What promotes effective time management can be summarized by simply listing a few of the characteristics of ideal meetings presented in Chapter 1:

- A clear understanding in advance of what will be expected from each participant

- A commitment to coming prepared

- A clear written agenda that is visible to all participants

- A commitment to respect each other's time

- Ground rules pertaining to focus, minimizing distractions, and leaving the room

It may not be necessary to say very much about what impairs effective use of time because this will simply be the reverse of what has been listed above. That is, effectiveness in budgeting time will invariably be weakened when participants come unprepared, are unclear about the group's agenda or their individual responsibilities, allow each other to be interrupted or distracted, and fail to respect the time of the other members present. But how to restore effective time management when that effectiveness is lost may not be quite so obvious.

In any given situation, there are usually many tools available. In Chapter 7, no fewer than 25 conflict prevention and intervention alternatives are explored in detail. As we turn now to look at some of the common challenges to time management at IEP meetings, we touch briefly on a few of those 25 intervention options. It bears emphasizing that effective meeting management and conflict prevention go very much hand in hand; a great many conflicts will be minimized or avoided by effectively managing the meetings. Conversely, and as mentioned before, many a conflict has its roots in a poorly run meeting.

Before talking about intervention strategies, let's assume that all team members

1. Know why the particular meeting is being held

2. Know in advance what they are expected to do or bring

3. Have a clear, written agenda

4. Have established agreed-upon ground rules

5. Have taken steps to minimize distractions (cell phones are off, a "do not disturb" sign is in place, calls are being held, and so on)

If a team has done these few things, it has already gone a long way toward preventing many of the potential challenges to efficient time management. They will also have done something else that can be extremely valuable: By first agreeing on ground rules, they can reference back to those rules whenever the need should arise.

Common Challenges and Intervention Options

A few of the commonly encountered challenges to effective use of time in the IEP environment include the following:

- Members arrive late.

- Members leave the room during the meeting.

- Presenters are excessively detailed, giving more information than is needed.

- Members go off on tangents, giving information that is not really relevant.

- Members are side-talking or busy with other things.

While the specific scenarios may differ greatly, the intervention options that can be most helpful are often exactly the same. In any of these scenarios, team members can **remind each other of the ground rules** and encourage a recommitment. Thus the chairperson (or any member) could say something like, "Excuse me, team, we agreed earlier that we would do our best to stay on task, knowing that our time is very limited today. How are we doing with that so far?" As another possibility, a member could **share the conflict** by expressing his or her own feelings. In this regard, the person could say something like, "Team, I am feeling a little concerned as I watch the time going by and see how much is still on our agenda for today." A member can **confront the group** (hopefully gently and kindly, in "we" rather than "you" terms): "I wonder if we may be getting a little off task right now." Any member can **share a good intention**, perhaps by saying, "Mr. Jones, I really want to understand all that you are sharing with us," and then **refocus** by saying something like, "Could I ask you to summarize the key points you want us to see?"

Different people may, individually, feel more comfortable with some of these approaches than with others, and it is certainly important that they be sincere and use their own words. Most of us have heard the familiar expression, "An ounce of prevention is worth a pound of cure." If a team does a good job of setting the stage before the meeting begins, many of the common challenges are unlikely to happen at all, or at least not very often. If and when they do arise, any of the options presented above could be appropriate and effective. Using such intervention alternatives may feel a little awkward at first, but with a little practice (maybe before the meeting and to an empty chair), they will soon become easy, comfortable, and even second nature.

Managing Emotion

If participants begin to feel any negative emotions, such as feeling overwhelmed, hurt, fearful, disrespected, frustrated, or a sense of injustice, such emotions can easily become obstacles to successful participation for the remainder of the meeting. Like a great big wall that suddenly goes up, if someone feels upset or offended, negative emotions can prevent them from hearing and productively responding to whatever it is that comes next. While it is easy to say and even agree, "Let's not get emotional" or "Let's not take things personally," this may not be very helpful in practice. The fact is that we are all *feeling* beings. Our emotions are alive and well at all times, and they must be respected and worked *with,* rather than hidden, suppressed, and worked against—at least if we hope to preserve a collaborative effort. The emotional side of living is the subject of future chapters, so for now, let's just briefly address the issue as it relates to meeting management.

All team members need to be alert to the feelings that the other team members will sometimes have. Feeling overwhelmed, stressed, confused, or pressured is common. Feeling intimidated, uncomfortable, disrespected, or belittled is (hopefully) rare but certainly not unheard of—and perhaps even to be expected from time to time. It is therefore essential to understand the importance of acknowledging, respecting, and even *encouraging* emotional expression and for several good reasons:

1. To provide an atmosphere of safety, caring, and mutual respect

2. To clear the blocks to working together cooperatively

3. To support the shared interests of having one's say and being heard

In recognizing the importance of supporting feelings, it is also important to distinguish between them (as emotions) and the perceptions, beliefs, or allegations that go with them. For example, imagine that Mrs. Smith is upset with a teacher and feels disrespected because she believes the teacher doesn't care what she has to say. The team can fully support her feeling disrespected (which is not to say that she *is* disrespected) without necessarily supporting her perception that the teacher doesn't care. One way a team member could express concern and **acknowledge** Mrs. Smith's feelings is by saying, "I sense that you are really unhappy with us right now, Mrs. Smith. Can you help us understand what has happened?" By encouraging her to express her feelings and perceptions openly, the team provides an atmosphere of caring and respect and provides the greatest probability of clearing the air and restoring their ability to work together in real partnership.

Of course, it is important that any such expression of feelings be productive and that it doesn't take too much time or lead the team too far off track. The purpose is always to maintain collaboration toward consensus in achieving the best possible IEPs for the children. What follows is a list of options that can help teams restore their spirit of collaboration and partnership if at any time it seems to be threatened.

Safeguarding a Collaborative Process

1. **Remind the team of its common goal** and interest: the best IEP for the child.

2. **Explore interests:** You must have good reasons for that; tell us some of them. That seems important to you; help us understand why. Say some more about that; in what ways would that be helpful?

3. **Clarify areas of agreement:** We all want what is best for the child. Nobody wants to go to a hearing if it can be avoided. We all want to make good use of our time. We all want to do what's right.

4. **Reframe negatives into more neutral statements:** "He never follows through" could be rephrased as "You'd want to be able to trust that the plan would really be implemented."

5. **Avoid big words** and unclear acronyms; clarify when necessary.

6. Watch the unspoken process (body language, facial expressions, tones of voice).

7. **Watch for mental or emotional overload;** "when in doubt, check it out" by asking how a teammate is feeling. (Take a break if necessary or ask the person how the group can be most helpful.)

8. If unproductive communication styles are being demonstrated, **support feelings, share the conflict, and remind of ground rules.**

9. Knowing that participants will sometimes feel lost, rushed, disrespected, or outnumbered, **acknowledge and support** those feelings. ("I might feel that way, too, in your shoes.")

10. **Make an agreement** to speak up if at any time members have bad feelings that seem to be interfering with working together.

Promoting Goal Achievement

To ensure that the group accomplishes the goals of the particular IEP meeting, some helpful options to include in the toolbox are

- *Play with the time shape* of proposals. For example, "How about for a month we try it and see, and if it doesn't work, we can reconvene the team and see what else might work better?" This time-limited approach can very often promote progress when the group would otherwise remain stuck. (It is often easier to agree to something as a short-term trial, as opposed to a long-term commitment.)

- Perhaps *build in guarantees* and contingencies. People usually resist ideas that they don't trust. One way around this is to make agreements about contingencies ("If that happens, then . . ."). For example, imagine that a teacher opposes keeping Johnny in his classroom because he believes that Johnny's disruptive behavior will continue. Perhaps he *would* agree to keep him if the team assures him that "If Johnny does that again, then we will all be ready to look at an alternate placement."

Sometimes, despite the best of efforts and intentions, the group may be unable to reach consensus. When this happens, the members should first try and clarify why that might be. Is it that they need more information? Is it that they disagree about the information that they have? Is it that misunderstandings or strong emotions have arisen? Once the nature of the obstacle is made clear, it will often also become clear how best to proceed, and the best way is always, whenever possible, to *make agreements about the disagreements*. For example, consider the following:

Obstacle: We seem to be stuck over this issue of whether additional testing is really necessary.

Agreement: What if we get advice from the reading specialist and then make our decision? [defer pending further information]

Obstacle: Some of us clearly believe that Johnny should have a laptop, while some of us think that an AlphaSmart could work even better.

Agreement: What if we give him an AlphaSmart for, say, a month and see how he does? Then we would have good reason to try something else, like a laptop, if he is not making progress. Does that seem like a possible solution? [play with the time shape of a proposal]

Obstacle: Team, it seems clear that we are not in agreement about whether extended school services are really necessary.

Agreement: What would you think about leaving this part undecided for now and talking more about this at our next meeting? [defer pending further thought and discussion]

Resolving Impasse

Impasse is a fancy word negotiators use when the parties are stuck and discussions seem to be going nowhere. There are two main types of impasse: momentary (when agreement may still be possible today) and fatal (when it really is clear that agreements are not going to be reached, at least under the present circumstances). A few options to consider for resolving impasse follow:

Momentary Impasse (agreement may still be possible today)

1. Confess and invite suggestions from the group. ("We seem to be kind of stuck right now—any suggestions for how we might move forward?")

2. Make the implicit explicit. Encourage the participants to verbalize and clarify (without discussion at this point) what they see as the obstacles—interests, feelings, expectations, assumptions, perceptions, and so on. ("Would it make sense to go around the table and just hear from each person what we see as the obstacles to our consensus today?")

3. Review the decision-making criteria. ("What do you all think would be our best way of approaching this issue? On what basis do you think we should make this decision?")

4. Retrace the day's progress to reestablish a positive outlook. ("May I take a minute to summarize what we have agreed so far?")

5. Review the shared risks of leaving the matter unresolved versus the shared benefits of reaching an agreement. ("I think we would all like to leave here with a sense of completion and an

(continued)

IEP in place for the next year, at least in an initial form. I know none of us wants to go away mad or have to go through the unpleasantness of a complaint investigation. Am I right?")

6. Take a break. ("I wonder if a 5-minute leg stretch might be a good idea. What do you all think?")

7. Have a private discussion if a member seems to need some additional support or a chance to let off steam. ("Mr. Smith, it would really help me to have a moment to clarify some things—just you and me. Would anyone object if we step out in the hall for just a minute or two?")

Fatal Impasse *(agreement is not possible under present circumstances)*

1. Make agreements about the disagreements. Recess pending further thought and discussion; continue after further evaluation or consultation with experts; continue the discussions with a different mix of people or in a different setting; request mediation.

2. Review what has been agreed and what remains undecided. Narrow the points in dispute, especially if a formal complaint or hearing request is likely to be filed.

3. When all else fails, the legal representative of the district (usually the chairperson) *may* have to exercise his or her authority to decide what the IEP will be, whether the team agrees or not. However, unless a violation of law would result by leaving the IEP incomplete, discussions can usually be continued at another time, and such sole decision making can be reserved for use only as a last resort.

CONCLUDING REMARKS

Let's look now at how best to conclude the IEP meeting. First, if time permits, the meeting can end with a brief and informal evaluation. *Asking is affirming,* as mentioned before, and the team can increase the likelihood of ending on a positive note by briefly discussing, "How do we all feel about today's meeting? Any recommendations for next time?" Similarly, all members should be given a chance to share any final remarks they would like to make. In this regard, the chairperson can ask, "Do any of you have anything else you would like to say before we end for today?" Such concluding remarks can serve several important purposes:

1. To maintain an atmosphere of respect and genuine interest

2. To provide an opportunity to learn from experience

3. To express and resolve negatives that could otherwise become obstacles

4. To share *positives* that might otherwise be kept hidden

5. To strengthen team spirit for the next meeting

FOLLOW UP

It can be very helpful to make some sort of outreach after the meeting, either later in the day or a few days later. This could involve a follow up between the chairperson and any member of the team, with such questions as, "How do you think the meeting went? Did you feel heard and included? Anything you didn't get a chance to say? Any thoughts or suggestions?"

While time may not permit extensive and *routine* follow up—and it will not always be necessary to do so—it is important to maintain an open door for contact between meetings if and when such contact would be helpful. This can be especially appropriate and valuable when a participant has left the meeting with bad feelings. Negativity tends to fester and grow, and the sooner the team can work it through, the better for all involved. Any member of the team can and should reach out if such a situation develops. If people have bad feelings but are not talking about them directly with the others who are involved, it's a safe bet that they are doing *something else* with those feelings—probably not as productive. In later chapters, more is said about emotions and how to resolve bad feelings that may arise. For now, we can conclude this chapter by simply emphasizing that, just as with many a conflict, many a bad feeling is prevented by a well-planned and well-run meeting.

Chapter 3

Achieving Collaboration and Consensus

C hapter 1 presents a three-fold vision of the IEP team and emphasizes that, under federal law, the team is intended to work together in a decision-making *partnership.* Yet IEP team members have generally been given little or no specific training in the process of collaborative decision making. They have been given very little to help them understand what it is, how to do it, and what to do when problems arise. It is from this very specific niche of identified need—how to actually manifest the vision of collaboration in the IEP environment—that this book and the training from which it arose have come about.

It has been said, "The truth is simple; it is not always easy," and the simple vision of the IEP team is certainly far from easy when it comes to putting it into practice. In the realm of special education, there are so many laws and policies, procedures and timelines, papers and reports, personnel and resources, agencies and authorities, tools and technologies, and so on. Small wonder that training in the process of collaboration has often been neglected. Yet, collaboration leading to consensus is the very process that must be safeguarded in the IEP environment.

DEFINITIONS

It can be very helpful to look to the dictionary as a starting point in any effort of understanding. If we look up *collaboration,* we will probably find something like

Collaboration: Working together toward common objectives

And if we look up *consensus,* we will find something like

Consensus: An opinion held by all or most; general agreement

Some people believe that consensus requires unanimity—agreement by *all* members of the group—but this is not necessarily so. Instead, teams can have consensus even with disagreement but *only* if the dissenting members are willing to support the decision of the group even when their individual choices differ. As an example, I personally may think it best that Danny be placed in a self-contained classroom, rather than remaining in the general classroom with a teacher's aide. My own professional judgment is that his behaviors are too disruptive, the demands on the classroom teacher are too great, and the risk of aggressive behavior is too high. However, the group clearly seems to think that with more time and a behavior intervention plan, Danny will be successful in the general classroom. Although I don't agree with the conclusion of the group as a whole, I will support the decision and be part of the consensus. If, on the other hand, I *strongly* disagreed and could not in good faith support the decision, then I would object and consensus would not yet be possible. Further time and discussion would be required. The point here is that there can be consensus even with disagreement, provided that the disagreeing member can remain supportive of the decision of the team as a whole.

As a means of bringing collaboration and consensus into sharper focus and understanding how they differ from other decision-making options, consider this hypothetical scenario. Imagine what might happen if we were to throw half a dozen people into a room, lock the door, and tell them that they can't come out until they have a completed IEP. It is safe enough to assume that they are going to do *something*. They are going to do their decision making *somehow*, and if they are not working together collaboratively, what are they likely to be doing instead? There's no such thing as doing nothing. What then are the most common alternatives to working collaboratively toward consensus? Well, the whole gamut of options falls under one heading: *adversarial approaches*.

ADVERSARIAL APPROACHES

Adversarial approaches include a full spectrum from silent withdrawal to violence and even war. The common element uniting all of them is "againstness," meaning working in opposition rather than in cooperation. Although we will not very often see the extreme forms of opposition in our locked room full of IEP team members, we *will* often see some of the less extreme forms of adversarial decision making. These will include

- **Withdrawal:** Simply failing to appear and participate in meetings

- **Passivity:** Silently going along with the crowd, while secretly harboring disagreement, disinterest, mistrust, or resentment

- **Debate:** Advancing and defending a conclusion already reached but not really sharing ideas or being open to alternative views

- **Hostility:** Raising voices, calling names, casting blame, making threats

Formal complaints and due process hearings can certainly be added to the list of adversarial approaches. While this is not to suggest that they are wrong or inappropriate, it must be recognized that formal complaints and due process hearings are both "me against you" methods of problem solving. They are adversarial, not cooperative.

In contrast, *mediation,* now specifically provided under federal law, is a collaborative alternative that can be used when the team just can't seem to come out of that locked room without agreement. In the specific language of the federal Office of Special Education Programs (OSEP),

> [Changes in the law,] including provisions that require that mediation be available to parents, were designed to save money and reduce discord by encouraging parents and educators to work out their differences using nonadversarial means.
> —http://www.abt.sliidea.org/Reports/FSI_FinalRpt.doc

Truly, if we are not working together cooperatively, we are certainly working against each other adversarially. But what's wrong with making decisions by adversarial methods? What's wrong with defending my position, especially if I know I am absolutely right? Why not just forget about all this collaborative mumbo-jumbo and do it in any way that works? Well, let's look more closely at the issues involved.

Implications of Adversarial Approaches

If a group, any group, makes its decision by adversarial means, what are the implications? There are several, and they are universal. Adversarial decision making will always be characterized by the following downsides:

- It is inherently competitive, with winners and losers.

- It precludes the possibility of synergism (the sum greater than the parts).

What happens to team spirit and effectiveness when, within a team, there are winners and losers? What do those members feel, think, and do when they believe that they have lost? Don't they tend to feel bad and to withdraw their energy and enthusiasm from the group?

If they don't believe that their own voices have been heard and respected, they are unlikely to support the decisions made by the group. Furthermore, when any member stands apart from the team as a whole unit, that wonderful possibility of synergism starts to become eroded. No longer does the team live the vision of shared information, shared decision making, and shared implementation. The group becomes crippled, and while it may still function, it does so less effectively. And who ultimately suffers when the group loses its strength and potential in this way, if not the children whose educations lie in the hands of the IEP team?

Having considered the alternatives to collaboration, what about the alternatives to consensus? Indeed, collaboration and consensus go hand in hand, and their interrelationship becomes very apparent with a closer look at the alternatives to consensual decision making. If teams are *not* making their decisions through general agreement (i.e., consensus), how then are they making them? The IEP team thrown into a locked room and required to stay put until it emerges with an IEP will surely use one decision-making method or another. It will almost certainly use one of the following three.

Majority Rule

The first alternative might involve discussing the issues for as long as they like and then taking a vote and letting the majority rule. The American culture holds its election-based political structure in very high esteem. Why not simply require that IEP teams act in accordance with their majorities? What limitations, if any, would electoral decision making have? Well, a vote always

- **Results in winners and losers:** As noted above, several things can happen to a team when some of its members see themselves on the losing end. Among these are that the outvoted members may harbor ill will, may become passive and apathetic, and may withdraw from future participation.

- **Leaves some viewpoints not addressed:** When a group decides by election, a number of significant issues may become silenced by vote, rather than explored and incorporated through continued investigation and discussion. Thus, some possibly good ideas will be overlooked, and some valid concerns or opposition may be bypassed to the detriment of the final decision.

- **Precludes the likelihood of synergism:** The wonderful potential of a group to maximize its potential wisdom and effectiveness will be eroded when only some, but not all, contribute to the decision.

- **Risks limited support:** Without having a say in the final decision of the group, the outvoted members are less likely to help implement the decisions reached by the majority.

If all this is true, did the American founding fathers make a big mistake to establish this great nation based on free elections and *not* as a consensus-based government? Well, what would it look like if every decision ever made by Congress, the Supreme Court, the city, county, and state had to be made by the consensus of all citizens? How much time would it require to get all citizens in unanimous or even general agreement? How efficient could such a system be? Obviously, the information required to make wise decisions would be far beyond the time and abilities of the average individual; a more practical and less demanding system had to be developed. The downside of consensus is that it requires information, commitment, cooperation, and *time*. It can be unwieldy in a large and very diverse group, but it works beautifully in the small-group setting with positive team spirit, dedicated and informed individuals, and a more limited range of focus. It can work supremely well in the IEP environment, to the benefit of all involved.

Dictatorship

Okay, so perhaps it can now be agreed that IEPs should not be decided by vote. What then are the other options? Well, another long-established model of decision making other than by consensus is dictatorship. (Perish the thought!) Historically speaking, the dictator may have been a king, queen, or other ruler, who may have been very kind, wise, and generous or very possibly quite the opposite. In the olden days of special education, the school principal or another figure of authority would decide what would be best for any particular child who had special educational requirements. While that decision maker may have chosen to consult with teachers, resource personnel, or parents, the final decision rested ultimately with the principal or the superintendent, the courts, or some other authoritarian figure.

Most Western nations have a great distaste, culturally, for the very concept of dictatorship because they value and respect the freedom and inclusion of the individual. But let's remain objective for the moment and consider the point that one option for the IEP team locked in the room is to have just one single person decide what the IEP will look like and then tell (not ask) the other members what that child's educational program will be. Certainly this is not, under federal law, the way the IEP team is intended to function. It is certainly not a decision-making *partnership.*

Of course, dictatorship may be more or less benign, meaning kind and well-intentioned, and dictators may function more or less autocratically. That is, they may rely entirely on their own judgment, or they might include the advice and agreement of others. Yet whenever a group makes decisions by dictatorship, the predictable outcome is exactly the same as before:

- **Results in winners and losers:** Some of the members' views are supported, while others' are overruled by the decision that was made.

- **Leaves some viewpoints not addressed:** There will again be a number of issues that are silenced without having been explored and incorporated. Good ideas may be overlooked and valid concerns may be bypassed.

- **Precludes the likelihood of synergism:** Only one person or perhaps a few, but certainly not all, have contributed to the final decision.

- **Risks limited support:** The members whose views are not represented in the decisions may not help to implement the decisions that are made.

Rule by the Vocal Minority ("The Big Dogs")

While IEP teams functioning under dictatorships may seem farfetched, this last decision-making alternative, rule by the vocal minority, or "the big dogs," is not rare at all. While few may ever have heard of it, it is definitely a method that can often be seen wherever groups are making decisions. It looks something like this: When a group is trying to decide what to do for lunch, one or another of the most outspoken members will say, "Let's get a pizza" or "Let's go to the Stumble Inn." Then another member or two will chime in, "Yeah, great!" and the next thing they know, the group is heading for the parking lot and on their way. When groups decide by the big dog method, the most vocal members persuade and the others just follow along. It is so common that we may fail to recognize it; and it's quick, and it's easy, and it seems to work—or does it? What are the implications? Well, curiously, the results are exactly the same as before:

- *Results in winners and losers*
- *Leaves some viewpoints not addressed*
- *Precludes the likelihood of synergism*
- *Risks limited support*

In addition, the big dog method may fail to recognize the *true* majority, and it may steer the group without reflecting the best wisdom within the group. Beware the big dogs! The best way to guard against them is to be sure that all members have had a say and to check out whether those who haven't spoken really do concur with those who have. In other words, "when in doubt, check it out." The group can always pause and ask whether there really is consensus when its more vocal members speak out. In the example of going to lunch, the chairperson (or any member) can simply ask, "Okay, sounds like some of us want to go the Stumble Inn—does everyone agree with that? Mary, how about you?" Yes, it takes more time to do it this way, but it is the only means of ensuring a true consensus.

Is it realistic to think that groups can always function collaboratively and reach consensus? Is this perhaps too idealistic in an arena as time-stretched, as emotionally charged, and as diverse as the IEP environment? Well, collaboration *is* possible most of the time, and consensus is increasingly possible when teams understand not only what it is and why it is important but also what steps they can take to get there. It all becomes much more realistic and attainable when they understand how to work effectively through the obstacles and challenges that typically arise.

WHEN CONSENSUS DOES NOT SEEM POSSIBLE

When, despite all reasonable efforts, consensus does not seem possible, it is important to clarify *why* this is so. Is it because the team does not yet have enough information to make its decisions? Is it that the information is conflicting and the team members need further investigation or clarification? Is it that tempers have risen, feelings have been hurt, or fears have come up that have blocked their ability (or willingness) to think clearly and maintain a cooperative stance? In other words, before a team loses its collaborative spirit, the members can try to understand what the hold up is all about. Armed with that awareness, they can often *collaboratively and consensually* decide how to move forward once again.

As mentioned in Chapter 2, team members can make agreements about their disagreements. The standard options whenever teams feel stuck are to

1. Defer pending further information

2. Delay pending further thought and discussion

3. Defer to an expert, trusting his or her best judgment

As mentioned before, consensus does not always require unanimity. Teams can have consensus with *general* agreement even when all members do not *individually* agree. The key, however, is an attitude of respect for the group as a whole and a commitment by all members to support the cooperative efforts of the team and not to obstruct or undermine when their personal views are not reflected in the outcome. If this sounds like double talk, it really is not. It merely urges teams to strive for consensus, to respect collaboration and sharing, to make time for listening to the feelings and opinions of all group members, and to reserve taking an adversarial role for those hopefully very rare times when it really is necessary. Taking the time for a little more discussion, for a little more thought, for perhaps another opinion or two—these kinds of things will lead to consensus most of the time.

Occasionally, there may be circumstances under which the committee chair, or another person who legally represents the school district, must shift roles and become the sole decision maker for the IEP team. This should only be necessary when a legal deadline would otherwise be missed or when the group would otherwise violate a provision of the law or exceed its legal authority. Such a shift in roles, from a facilitator of collaboration to a sole decision maker, should be very rare and all the more so when the group really understands its obligations to the child and commits to working together collaboratively. Let's look now at the means by which collaboration can be supported despite the many challenges unique to the IEP arena.

PRINCIPLED NEGOTIATION

The term *principled negotiation* refers to a system developed by Roger Fisher and William Ury of Harvard University. Their landmark work was presented in the book *Getting to Yes,* published in 1981, which has become a key reference for negotiators, facilitators, mediators, and all those professionally involved in conflict prevention and resolution. The ideas are taken a step further in the sequel by

William Ury, *Getting Past No.* Their system works, and it works supremely well in providing a simple yet powerful avenue for reaching the goal of achieving consensus in the IEP environment. The model distinguishes between position-based and interest-based bargaining. In this simple dichotomy lies a great deal of what is needed for promoting effective teamwork while minimizing conflict.

Simply stated, most arguments involve two or more people who have become stuck at the level of conflicting *demands.* Demands are essentially the "what we want" and are the positions we have taken. Examples abound in the IEP environment: "I demand that my child be kept in the general classroom." "I insist that this child be removed from my classroom." "I want you to get him a laptop computer." "All she needs is a teacher's aide." "What he needs is more support in the home." "What she needs is an attitude adjustment!" Like wheels spinning in sand without moving forward, people often latch onto positions and then fight to be heard and to get what they say they want. These are all examples of position-based negotiation and can look very much like a game of tennis: I send you my idea and you send me your idea, back and forth over a dividing net into our separate courts, with nobody really listening, neither of us feeling heard or understood, and no real progress being made.

The Tug-of-War Alternative

The analogy of a game of tug-of-war can be helpful, where people are pulling on opposite ends of a rope: one side wins when they pull the other side through the mud or when the other side gives up and lets go of the rope. Another possible outcome might be if the rope breaks and they *all* fall down. Win–lose, give up, or break are the only options of the game. From the realm of analogy, let's return now to the committee room table. It is easy to see three possible outcomes that parallel the tug-of-war analogy:

1. The argument ends when someone's opinions are overruled by the group or by some figure of authority (the winners) and that

person then feels defeated and dragged through the mud (with lots of negative side effects, to be sure).

2. The argument ends when someone gives up in disagreement, disgust, and despair—one side stops discussing the issues and in effect lets go of the rope (lots of negative side effects here, too).

3. The argument ends when the rope breaks and the process of negotiation breaks down—the participants withdraw into their separate camps, end their participation with the team, and/or file a formal complaint or a request for a due process hearing.

Surely there must be a better way! So long as people fight for their positions at the expense of true sharing and understanding, they all lose: Nobody wins unless everybody wins, which really *is* possible when they know how. Principled negotiation offers that chance.

In contrast to arguing for positions, the model encourages decision makers to first seek to understand the *interests* behind those positions, what it is they (and the other parties) are *trying to achieve* with the positions they have taken. What is it they hope to accomplish if given what they demand—on both sides of the table?

> If you are trying to change their minds, the starting point is to figure out where their minds are now. (*Getting to Yes*, p. 44)

The Fourfold Model

Principled negotiation has four cornerstones:

1. **People:** Who are the people and what do they bring to the table in terms of feelings, attitudes, past experiences, expectations, and so on?

2. **Interests:** What goals and objectives are they seeking to achieve by whatever it is they are asking for? *Why* do they want what they say they want?

3. **Options:** What possibilities exist to satisfy those interests—from the very broad range of available resources?

4. **Criteria:** On what basis will they decide which of their many options is best?

In applying this simple model to the IEP environment, it is not difficult to fill in the blanks.

People Issues

Who are the people and what do they bring? Well, in broad terms, IEP teams include parents, teachers, resource personnel, and administrators (and sometimes the student). In some regards, they all have much in common: they share a concern for the well-being of the child, and they have a number of similar and compatible interests (which are explained in a moment). But they also have a great many differences.

The parents may have *feelings* of apprehension and mistrust and of being out of their element when attending meetings with a room full of school staff. They may harbor strong feelings concerning their child and his or her educational challenges. Toes may be inadvertently stepped on when some of those deep feelings are accidentally triggered. New and troubling feelings may emerge as a result of the latest test results or school reports. These feelings may include guilt, sadness, loss, fear, anger, injustice, and so on. Of course, strong *positive* feelings may arise as well, in response to favorable reports and observations or support and encouragement from other team members. In either event, though, and in probable contrast to the other members of the IEP team, it is the parents who are likely to have the strongest emotions. They stand in a unique position with regard to the child—a position no one else on the team can ever really share.

The parents will also bring a different *mind set* that can set them apart from the rest of the IEP team. This mind set will include their perceptions, beliefs, expectations, interpretations, and assumptions, and it is likely to be based on their past experience with school personnel. Very often, their child has not conformed to the school's expectations in the past, and the parents may come with a history of negative interaction with school officials—including other IEP teams! The parents may also differ in their levels of education and *personal styles,* including verbal skills, degrees of confidence, and approaches to negotiating—cooperative verses adversarial, active or more passive, detail-oriented versus more broad brush, and so on.

School officials, each and every one of them, will also bring feelings, mind sets, and personal styles. Some will be more outspoken, some more supportive and understanding, some more patient, and so on. And all of these people, parents included, will have their own *other* responsibilities, the things they are not doing while taking time to attend the IEP meeting. They each have their own constituents, the people they must answer to as to how they are spending their time and what they are accomplishing with the IEP team. All of these variables, multiplied by the number of people on the team, augmented by the circumstances and pressures of that particular week or day—*all* of these will fill up the grab bag of characteristics that constitute the people issues for that IEP team at that particular team meeting. Let's look a little more closely at the differences among the school staff because, while having certain similarities, they are definitely not all the same.

The principal (or the principal's designee) is probably the chairperson of the team. He—or let's say she—is responsible for managing the meeting and seeing to it that its legal obligations are fulfilled. She is probably the only team member authorized to commit the spending of district funds, which are usually much more limited than the team would often like. She answers to the superintendent, and if any errors, omissions, or violations of law are discovered or any allegations of wrongdoing are made, it is the principal (or the designee) who must step forward and give an account.

The general classroom teachers have a different set of constraints. As mentioned before, someone has to be covering their classes while they are away at IEP meetings; the longer the meeting, the more behind they may be getting, and the more pressure and stress they may be feeling. In addition, most general classroom teachers have perhaps 20 or more *other* students to be concerned about, and it is often very challenging for them to accommodate the needs of their one or two (or more) children with special educational needs. After all, they are general and not special education teachers. It is a rare school or district that is flush with time and money. Most are stretched to the maximum, and the general classroom teachers invariably feel it.

The special education teachers also face circumstances that may be different from those of the other members of the team. They are committed to the welfare of the children entrusted to them, and yet they are often frustrated by the difficulties involved in finding the support, the staffing, and the resources to give the children what they know is most needed. They may also be stretched to provide adequate time and attention to the many children they serve. These characteristics usually apply to the various resource personnel as well—occupational and physical therapists, speech pathologists, diagnosticians, counselors, and so on. Many of these people serve more than one school, thus having the added challenge of time to travel and the responsibility of keeping other appointments at perhaps far distant places.

Without even beginning to look at the unique circumstances of the particular *individuals* involved, there are obviously many challenging circumstances that the members of the team will often, in their own and perhaps different ways, be working to manage. These challenges are apart from any health issues, family issues, financial or employment issues, or other potential stressors that will also be relevant aspects of the people issues at the table on any given day. This picture is not meant to be gloomy nor to make excuses. It is only meant to clarify the great many strands in the fabric that help make up the whole. Recognizing, or at least being open to, these many features and variables can go a long way toward promoting the respect and understanding so vital to maintaining strong teams.

Interests

Interests, perhaps more than any other aspect of the fourfold model, are what make principled negotiation such a powerful means of moving discussions from an exchange of demands to a cooperative problem-solving venture. As mentioned before, the interests are the objectives, often hidden, that underlie whatever it is that people say that they want. Some examples are

I demand that my child stay in the general classroom, despite his disruptive behavior, because I fear that making him "different" will be very damaging to his self-esteem. My interest is in preserving a positive sense of self.

I demand that this child be given further testing because I believe that the latest scores are misleading and that decisions will otherwise be made that are not really best for him. My interest is in seeing that an accurate basis exists for the decisions the committee will make.

I demand that the teacher be reprimanded because I perceive her behavior as injurious and want to see it stopped. My interest is in protecting the children who may otherwise suffer unjustly.

Notice that all of these interests are commendable! Who can deny that self-esteem, accuracy, and safety are all worthwhile values? Yet, at the same time, all of these interests are also at least partly *subjective.* They are all based on beliefs, fears, expectations, and assumptions—none of which may be wholly valid, but most of which will have at least *some* elements of truth—and all of them represent the feelings and perceptions of one or more of the team members. If only for that reason alone, they should be worthy of care and respect.

So long as the team argues at the level of positions, the probability is strong that tempers will rise, team spirit and cooperation will weaken, and a request for a due process hearing might ultimately result. But watch how quickly the picture can change if members look beyond positions and begin to see *interests* as their real topic of concern. They can then become curious about why someone wants what it is they say they want. What would it accomplish? How would it be helpful? What problems might it solve? The list of such exploratory questions goes on and on, but it begins with a recognition that

1. Team members are not adversaries. They are partners in a joint problem-solving challenge, always for the benefit of the child.

2. Whatever a member wants must be based in *some* good reasons. The team can be curious and seek to explore and understand them.

3. By understanding *why* a person wants what he or she wants, perhaps other equally good or even better solutions will become clear.

4. If nothing else, the members can choose to respect the rights, the dignity, and the feelings of everyone on the team, and at all times they can seek not to criticize but to be open and to understand. Only in so doing can the strength of the team be maintained.

The list of possible questions to ask for exploring interests is really an endless one. Because this topic may be very new to some readers, it might be helpful to provide some examples of the specific words one can use. In a moment, such a list of possible questions will be presented. By all means, add to it in any way you wish. Find the words that fit best for you, and yet recognize the importance of seeing not the tip of the iceberg (the demands) but all that lies hidden beneath it (the interests).

Speaking of what is hidden, it is important to understand that we, as human beings, are not always *conscious* of our interests. I may want this service, that technological device, or that change to the IEP and yet have trouble articulating why that is until I start exploring my thoughts and feelings. Questions such as "What would it look like if we did it that way?" or "How would that be helpful?" or "Where do you see that leading us?"—any of these may be helpful when a simple "Why?" does not fully clarify the issues.

Another point to consider is that people do not always feel safe to share their interests even when they are aware of them. This is especially likely if members do not see themselves as welcome, valued, and respected within the team. Thus, the reason I want my son to have a laptop may be that my spouse told me, in very strong terms, that I had better see to it that he gets one. If so, then one of my interests may be keeping peace at home and avoiding the risk of my spouse's anger or criticism. Am I likely to say so? Am I likely to announce to the group that the reason I want the IEP to look a certain way is because I fear the anger of my constituents (i.e., my spouse)? Not unless I am first aware of my feelings and thoughts and, second, willing to share them because I feel safe enough with my team.

Are there other fears that may not be immediately disclosed to the IEP team? Are there other interests that may be driving a member's decisions and yet not being openly discussed? Often there are, and these can include fears of appearing foolish (interest in being respected), fears of exceeding a budget (interest in staying within limits), fears of precipitating complaints or hearings (interest in avoiding unnecessary time and expense), and so on. Many of these might not be shared with the team, and yet the greater the ability of the team to maintain a spirit of openness, trust, and respect, the more likely all members *will* feel free to speak and to put on the table the issues to be resolved in order for consensus to emerge. The alternative is to play tug-of-war and remain stuck at the level of demands while harboring hidden agendas. And what are hidden agendas except those *interests* a person is unwilling to acknowledge or share? A commitment to mutual respect, true collaboration, and the best interests of the child will go far toward minimizing such limitations in the IEP team. The questions that follow can help clarify the underlying interests that may not always be apparent.

Questions that Probe for Underlying Interests

1. You must have good reasons for that; can you tell us some of them?

2. Can you help me understand where you're coming from?

3. How will that suggestion be helpful?

4. What do you see happening if we go that route?

5. Can you tell us more about that?

6. How do you think that will address the issue?

7. If we look down the road with that, what do you think it will look like?

8. What benefits could we expect if we did that?

9. In what ways could that be important?

10. And if we do that, then . . . ?

11. Why would you want to see that happen?

12. Why *not* do it the way she suggested? [i.e., the other person's way]

13. What would be wrong with trying it that way? [i.e., the other person's way]

14. What harm would come if we did it his way? [i.e., the other person's way]

15. How can we convince them that your idea is best?

Shared Interests and Shared Risks

Before moving on to the other two elements of principled negotiation, let's briefly address the issues of shared interests and shared risks. In every negotiation—that is, in every situation where people are discussing what it is they want and why—there will be interests that are shared and interests that differ. Many will depend on the specifics, but there are others that are just about universal. In terms of IEP teams, many of these shared interests come into focus when reviewing what characterizes good meetings (discussed in Chapter 1). Some of these shared interests include the following:

Shared Interests

1. Having a sense of achievement
2. Being a valued member of the group
3. Having a say in the decisions being made
4. Making good use of time
5. Starting and ending on time
6. Being heard and understood
7. Feeling welcome and respected
8. Feeling comfortable physically
9. Developing a good IEP
10. Ensuring the well-being of the child
11. Maintaining privacy and confidentiality
12. Looking good to constituents (absent family members or school officials)
13. Nurturing the future relationship of the teammates
14. Avoiding shared risks

The last point is a big one: **Avoiding a shared risk is always a common interest!** And what are some of those shared risks that team members would probably all like to avoid? Some are specific to the situation, but many are, again, almost universal. Team members would all usually prefer to avoid the following:

Shared Risks

1. Failing to complete their task

2. Developing an unwise IEP

3. Losing time off work or from other responsibilities

4. Having to meet again when not really necessary

5. Looking bad to constituents

6. Appearing foolish, being embarrassed, or losing face

7. Being judged, criticized, or rejected

8. Creating an unpleasant atmosphere

9. Having tensions escalate

10. Enduring a formal complaint or due process hearing

Again, a very important point to understand is that at all times, in all negotiations, at all meetings, *avoiding a shared risk is always a common interest.* Very often, this simple fact can provide the leverage needed to bring teams back into cooperation when they have become at odds. As examples, imagine one member saying to the group:

Team, I'm concerned that if we aren't time conscious, our meeting may run over. [shared interest in good use of time, and shared risk of extra time being needed]

Excuse me, Mr. Jones. I really want to understand the points you are raising—could you say that again in everyday terms? [shared interest in understanding, and shared risk of missing important points]

Maybe another series of tests would really clarify his reading level, which would then help us know what would be best. [shared interest in accurate information, and shared risk of deciding based on faulty information]

Although people often differ in the positions that they take, they can very often find common ground in their underlying interests. Once a team really understands the importance of finding those interests, the rest will often fall neatly into place.

Options

Think of options as a huge warehouse full of all the possible choices available as teams work to develop the best possible IEP for any particular child. These choices fall into such categories as

- Educational programming (what best serves this particular child)
- Staffing (teachers, aides, tutors, interpreters)
- Resource personnel (specialists, counselors, diagnosticians, and so on)
- Professional development (what new training would most assist staff)
- Settings (buildings, schools, classrooms)
- Technology (computers, reading and hearing supports, mobility aids, and so on)
- Time (before, during, and after school, extended school year)
- Community resources (medical, employment, transportation, and so on)
- Financial resources (what is needed and what sources are available)

How often do people get stuck in fears that they won't have what they need in order to do whatever it is they need to do? How many teams get stuck because they are unaware of the enormous range of options available to them? Most of the time, the possibilities are far greater than they realize, and by working together with others who are more "in the know," they can usually navigate their way through all the uncertainties and challenges to find meaningful answers to the problems at hand. Teams can always do this best by maintaining their invaluable team spirit and communication and by working together *collaboratively.*

A very helpful technique teams can use is *brainstorming*—the process of tossing out ideas (good, bad, or indifferent) while suspending judgment. Once the brainstorming session is completed, the members can then explore those many ideas and critique, accept, reject, or amend them one by one. The pitfall that people often fall into is doing their critiquing before they finish generating their ideas, and this puts the big kibosh on the group's felt freedom to be creative and expansive. It also makes for less efficient use of time.

A key element of option generation and exploration is changing "either/or" into "both/and." Instead of arguing for this idea versus that one (my way in opposition to yours), teams can maintain a perspective of looking for the value in both ideas and arriving at a conclusion that all can support. In this way, you get what you want and I get what I want—we both can win. When people compromise, they each usually get only part of what they want, but by collaborating toward consensus, they can often get *all* of what they want.

This may seem far-fetched to those who have not seen the phenomenal potential of groups working together in true collaboration and thereby developing the synergism mentioned before. There is a story that may serve to clarify how realistic this win–win possibility really is and what this problem-solving process can look like. It concerns two people arguing at the library.

THE CASE OF THE NOISY LIBRARY

Two men are quarreling in the library. One wants to open the window. The other wants to keep it closed. What could the librarian do to settle the conflict?

Obviously, this is a tug-of-war in which, at first glance, it would seem impossible for both parties to get what they want and walk away happy. But if the librarian applies principled negotiation and begins to explore the underlying interests, the options for settling the disagreement have a chance to emerge.

By asking such questions as why, what if, how might this help, and similar probing questions, the librarian may discover that one wants the window open because it is stuffy and he feels uncomfortable, and the other wants it closed because he doesn't want the breeze to blow his papers away. Once the librarian understands the interests, a solution becomes readily apparent: She can open the window in the next cubicle, which gives the one the fresh air that he wanted while preventing the breeze that the second wanted to avoid. A number of such scenarios are explored in some detail later in this chapter, specifically tailored to the IEP environment.

Criteria

This final element of principled negotiation simply refers to the basis upon which the team will make its decisions. This basis will usually include

- Legal requirements and district policies

- Test results and normative data

- Home and classroom observations

- Specialists' recommendations

Part of any group's assurance of achieving consensus will be the member's mutual understanding of *how* they will make their decisions! In other words, if the team members can agree that they will decide based on the criteria listed above, they will give those the greatest consideration. In contrast, if they believe that their decisions should be based on any one person's opinions or authority, or whoever is most coercive, or whatever is quickest and easiest, or any such lesser consideration, the probability of consensus is greatly diminished.

Awareness is a big part of this equation: Most groups have not yet spoken openly about how they will decide; they simply start talking as if their criteria were already established and agreed. If problems arise, this may be the very point they need to step back and revisit, perhaps by saying something like, "Team, we seem to be stuck on this point. Would it make sense to focus for a moment not on the issues themselves but on what kinds of factors should be most important as we try to answer this question?" In other words, at any time, the committee members can focus back onto the criteria, rather than the options, positions, or even interests, and this will often help them reopen their pathway toward progress. Similarly, they can always recommit that their decisions will *not* be based on a tug-of-war of opposing wills and demands.

A final thought about criteria: There are those that are relatively objective and not debatable. These would include test results, medical reports, and similar hard data (although there are almost always variables to make the hardest data subject to question and discussion). But there are other criteria that can be very much less objective and yet also important in any group's decision-making process. These include the best interests of the child (there can be lots of different perspectives on this top-of-the-list priority); they also include a sense of fairness for all members of the group (also a slippery slope). The point is that the members can choose to adopt such less objective criteria as important elements in their decision-making process. They can choose to make no decisions until all members agree that it is in the best interests of the child and that it is a decision they can all feel good about and support. These may be considered soft criteria and yet have many advantages that make them worth the time and effort required to achieve such a high level of consensus. The alternative is to risk having winners and losers, with all the downsides that usually go along.

Applying Principled Negotiation

Having presented the four basic elements of principled negotiation, we can now go a step further and apply this consensus-building model to some very specific (and real-life) scenarios in the IEP environment. In each example, the task will be to explore:

- What **people** issues probably exist?

- What **interests** might underlie the positions the different sides have taken (why they might want what they say they want)?

- What are a few **options** that might satisfy those interests?

- What **criteria** could they use?

THE CASE OF THE MISSING REPORT

The purpose of today's IEP team meeting is to discuss the possible need for extended school year services for Mary, so that she maintains her gains during the long summer break. At a previous IEP team meeting, it was agreed that the chairman would arrange for an assessment of Mary's current reading level. The chairman was out sick and got behind in his work, and he apologizes that no new testing was done. The parent is furious and becomes abusive, demanding that a whole battery of tests be given now to establish current performance levels. As tempers flare, one teacher recommends adjourning the meeting and reconvening at a later date. The speech pathologist says, "What if we just take a break?" How can this group restore collaboration and reach a consensus?

People

Who are the key players and what are the probable thoughts, feelings, and constraints that they bring to this experience? Well, we don't have a lot of information, so we may have to be creative and make a few assumptions.

It seems likely that all of them are busy. Perhaps the parent is thinking, "What a waste of time! I got special permission to take time off work, without pay, to attend this meeting, and now we can't even do what we need to do because of his incompetence!" She may be feeling frustrated, discouraged, and a sense of injustice. If she has had negative experiences with school officials in the past, that frame of reference may be "fanning the fires" at this present meeting, perhaps more than is really necessary or helpful.

The chairman might be thinking, "The testing was not really required, only discretionary. The information we need is available from other sources, such as the teachers' progress reports, so there was no real reason to postpone this meeting. If we decide that we still need further testing, we can still arrange for it." He may or may not be correct that the testing was not all that important, but either way, he will certainly feel differently than the parent.

Perhaps the teacher is thinking, "I am really uncomfortable with conflict and anger. I think we'd all feel better if we ended this right now." Her desire to end the meeting may have more to do with her own feelings of discomfort than any real need or danger.

The speech pathologist may be silently thinking, "I have three schools to visit today. I don't have time to come back again and again just because you all can't get your ducks lined up." She is probably feeling frustrated and perhaps nervous about keeping to her schedule. She may also be feeling irritated with this group.

In this scenario of the missing report, the wealth of negative thoughts and possibly intense feelings will certainly contribute to the climate of the meeting. How they are managed will have everything to do with whether collaboration is restored and whether or not consensus is ultimately achieved. As mentioned in the previous chapters, the challenges of every meeting include goal achievement, budgeting time, managing emotion, and safeguarding a collaborative process. It is easy to see how all of these may be required if this IEP meeting is to have a successful outcome (and a happy ending).

Interests

What interests probably underlie the positions that the group members have taken? Note that their very different *positions* are clearly stated in the very brief synopsis: do the testing as promised; do a whole battery of testing; overlook the testing; end the meeting and reconvene at another time; take a break.

What interest lies behind the parent demanding a whole battery of tests? Again, we will have to be a little creative and fill in a few blanks. No doubt she has an interest in promises being kept and expectations being met. She wants to see sufficient information available so that the team can make wise decisions. She wants to protect the rights and best interests of her child. She wants to make good use of time, and she wants her work schedule to be respected. Perhaps she wants some retribution for the school's neglect by having even more testing done now, an interest in justice being served. While the team may or may not agree with the positions she has chosen to take, they can probably find much to respect in all of her underlying *interests*.

The chairman's interests probably include having his apology accepted (for neglecting to arrange the testing); making good use of time, even without the testing; seeing some respect for his experience and professional judgment; being spoken to with respect rather than blame and attack; and also serving the best interests of the child.

The teacher's interests are probably to make good use of time, to avoid hostility, and to maintain a pleasant and cooperative atmosphere.

The speech pathologist's interests might be to find a way to deal with adversity without adding to her many responsibilities, to make good use of time and avoid postponement unless really necessary, and for the team members to get along with each other and achieve their team objectives.

It is not really difficult to take positions to their deeper level— from the tip of the iceberg (demands) to what lies underneath (the motivations). Exploring those underlying motivations (i.e., the interests) begins to shift the picture. It becomes so much easier to have understanding and even compassion for the good intentions behind the surface-level demands. It also becomes easier to expand the range of possibilities by which to resolve the issues and disagreements— in other words, to move from the one demand to the many possible options that might satisfy the underlying *interests*. Positions so often divide us, whereas interests usually unite us.

Options

What options are available to the IEP team in the case of the missing report? Perhaps the meeting could focus on the other issues on the table and defer the matter of reading skills until after further testing is done. Perhaps the team can agree that the information concerning reading is indeed available from other sources (home and classroom observations), and the meeting can move forward perfectly well without the testing being done at all. Perhaps a 5-minute break would help everyone calm down and recommit to working together as partners. Perhaps a short, private, and supportive meeting between one of the teachers and the parent would help. Perhaps an open apology from the chairman would help: "Mrs. Jones, I sincerely apologize for my oversight, and I can understand your frustration. I hope you'll forgive me. I do believe we can still make good progress today." There are always options and usually lots of them. If, indeed, after exploring the options, the consensus of the group members is that testing really is necessary for today's meeting, then of course they could also postpone and reconvene as one member had suggested.

Criteria

On what basis will the IEP team decide whether or not to continue the meeting or to postpone pending the results of further testing? Let's recall that the team's task for the meeting is to decide whether or not to provide Mary with extended school year services, so that her gains are not lost over the summer break.

In terms of *objective* criteria, the team cannot really make this decision without knowing Mary's current reading levels. The group will therefore have to decide whether it already has this necessary information (from other sources) or whether it will, in fact, require the data that can only come from additional and more current test reports.

In terms of *subjective* criteria, the team may be committed to making decisions only when all members feel satisfied that they have had a chance to share and contribute, and when all members can support the decisions made by the team. Note how such criteria differ from the more objective nature of normative test results. The team members may have set ground rules for their meeting, perhaps agreeing to respect the opinions and feelings of all members. Perhaps as part of their decision-making process about Mary's testing and the postponement of today's meeting, they could go around the table and hear briefly from each team member. In this way, they will avoid decision making by the vocal minority (the big dogs), while ensuring that each member receives the attention and respect that their team spirit both requires and deserves. Instead of debating as adversaries, they can share as decision-making *partners* and so collaborate toward consensus using both objective and subjective criteria.

THE CASE OF THE SPITTING IMAGE

Today's IEP team meeting has been specially called to decide whether Frank's disruptive behavior requires changes to his IEP. It seems that Frank has been spitting at other students in class. The general classroom teacher is adamant that she wants him out of her classroom after she received a threatening note from the parent whose child was spit on. Frank's father says that Frank is not really difficult to manage—he just needs a little extra attention. The principal (the committee chair) received an e-mail from the superintendent telling her she had better resolve this very quickly, as such behavior cannot be tolerated. How should this be resolved?

As in the first scenario, the people, interests, options, and criteria can be explored. Again, because not all of the history and details are revealed, we may have to make a few creative but reasonable assumptions.

People

The general classroom teacher probably has 20 other students to manage and finds Frank's behavior to be both a serious disruption and a heavy addition to the many responsibilities she has to handle. She may have little background in special education and may not have had much formal training in behavior management. She probably feels intimidated by the threatening note she received and perhaps fears having negative information in her personnel file that could affect her future employment. She may also fear that this could lead to a due process hearing or formal investigation, which could take up a great deal of her very limited time.

The principal may feel pressured by the superintendent to settle this matter and is probably also busy with other priority issues at the school. She may wish the general classroom teacher would just take care of this so she doesn't have to get involved.

The parent may know that Frank often uses inappropriate behavior as a way of getting attention, especially when he feels bored or frustrated. The parent may have had calls from neighbors or family members about similar "acting out." He may fear that Frank is becoming more and more separate from his peers and may feel embarrassed or even scared about this. He probably has a full-time job and perhaps several other children. He may hope the school can just take care of this because he does not know how and really can't handle much more stress and tension.

Interests

All of these team members share a common interest in developing a meaningful IEP. They all share an interest in their future relationship as team members. They will be working together for the next several years, and Frank depends on them all. They all share an interest in looking good to their constituents: father to mother and other children; father to extended family and neighborhood; teacher to principal; teacher to parents; teacher to future employers; principal to superintendent; superintendent to school board.

As mentioned previously, avoiding a shared risk is always a common interest. In this scenario, all team members want to avoid a breakdown of team spirit, participation, and cooperation. They would probably like to avoid an escalation of tensions with the parent of the child who was spit on and thus avoid the risk of a formal complaint or legal action in this regard. No doubt they would also like to avoid escalations with Frank's parents if the other members believe they really *must* remove Frank from the general classroom.

Options

A behavior assessment can be done, perhaps with the assistance of a behavior management specialist or other resource professional. A teacher's aide might be brought in to closely attend to Frank's needs and behavior in the classroom. The principal might help the general classroom teacher find support from other teachers who have had similar challenges in the past. The principal could also assure the teacher that no disciplinary action would be taken against her. The principal could phone the threatening parent and reassure her that the school is aware of the spitting behavior and is taking active steps to address it. The list of options goes on and on, but as long as the team members remain stuck at the level of conflicting demands, they may fail to recognize the possibilities that really do exist. After all, Frank is not likely to be the first child in history to have shown such behavior; surely with a little time and collaboration, this team, too, can successfully respond.

Criteria

Can the team members agree that they will not decide how to proceed based on conflicting wills and who shouts the loudest? Can they agree that intimidation and fears, from whatever sources, will not rule the decisions of the team? Can they recommit to mutual respect and understanding, while working together cooperatively in Frank's best interests? And can they formulate a plan that they will investigate this matter, trust the process, and make decisions based on the results of a behavioral assessment and the advice of their many expert resources?

The two scenarios we have now explored are very different in many ways. At the same time, they have much in common. By understanding the people involved, by moving from positions to interests, and then by exploring options and criteria, both teams can use principled negotiation as a means of moving forward.

What follows is a list of rhetorical questions team members can ask themselves, not only in the IEP environment but in any circumstances where conflict looms on the horizon (and even when it does not):

Questions for Applying Principled Negotiation

1. What are the different people probably thinking, feeling, assuming, or saying about each other? What past experiences might they be bringing that color their perceptions? [people issues]

2. What are the possible reasons why each person might want what they are asking for? What are their intentions, motivations, aspirations, or objectives? That is, what interests underlie their positions?

3. What questions could be asked to gain greater understanding of their positions? In other words, what questions will probe for their underlying interests? [e.g., Say some more about that. How might that be helpful? What do you see happening if we go that route?]

4. What are some benefits each side would achieve by restoring collaboration and reaching consensus? [shared interests]

5. What are some shared risks if the sides can not reach agreement?

6. What would help them begin to work toward an agreement? [respect, listening, understanding, openness]

7. What possible solutions (options) exist that might address their various interests?

8. What criteria are they using to resolve this issue? What can they agree should be the basis for their decisions?

9. Are they stuck in tug-of-war (exchanging demands in a contest of wills) or can they reaffirm a commitment to team effectiveness, common interests, and shared goals?

Armed with these and similar questions, any team can put principled negotiation to work and quickly see its benefits.

Part II

Conflict Resolution and Prevention

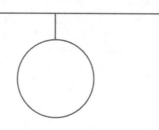

Chapter 4

Timelines and Behavior Trains

P art 1 explores the vision of the IEP team and presents a number of recommendations for managing IEP meetings in ways that promote both harmony and efficiency. Given an understanding of how important effective meeting management is for conflict prevention, it is time to move on to the second broad segment of this book: conflict prevention and resolution as a subject in itself. In doing so, it can be both helpful and enlightening to begin by considering the defining characteristics of conflict. There are two:

1. Opposition: Adversity, resistance, antagonism, as in "me against you" or "us against them"

2. "Bad" feelings: The negative feelings that *always* underlie the *choice* to resist or oppose (i.e., the choice to adopt the oppositional stance mentioned above)

Thus, wherever there is conflict in interpersonal relationships, there will always be negative emotions (such as disappointment, resentment, fear, hurt, and so on) *and* a behavioral choice to resist, reject, or otherwise oppose. Where there is no choice to oppose (as in friendship, togetherness, harmony, mutual respect, or collaboration), there is no conflict, although there *may* still be difference of opinion or disagreement, and there may even be bad feelings.

For example, if I like vanilla and you like chocolate, we can probably remain friends and respect our differences despite our differing views. On the other hand, if we are partners in an ice cream factory, trying to decide which flavor we will eliminate from production, such differences could easily develop into conflict. Why might that be? Why couldn't we respect our differences just as easily in either scenario? Well, theoretically we could, but in the factory, we are likely to have strong *feelings* associated with our positions, and unless we know how to maintain unity and cooperation in the face of our differences, conflict is likely to result.

Most people are very quick to move from strong feelings into opposition. It is not that they really have to move into opposition, but they usually do this so automatically that they may not be aware that they are doing it or that they have options. In the ice cream factory example, strong feelings may underlie the conflict, but as always, it is more the willingness to move into opposition that results in the conflict. If the people involved were honestly willing to respect their differences and continue to work together in true collaboration, conflict would never arise! If they were more attached to the wisdom and strength of their partnership, of their *team,* and less to their personal desires or to being right, wouldn't they paint very different pictures?

Collaboration was addressed in earlier chapters with an emphasis on the value of exploring underlying interests and remembering a shared commitment to the best IEP for the child. Let's look more closely now at the "steam that drives the train" and explore those unpleasant feelings that invariably underlie conflicts. A simple story can reveal a great deal.

THE STORY OF TWO FROGS

Two frogs fell into a pail of milk. The first frog was a pessimist. Saying to himself, "There is no hope;

there is no way out of here," he promptly sank to the bottom and drowned. The second frog was an optimist and kept saying to herself, "I know there's a way out. I know I can find it!" And she kicked and splashed and kicked and splashed, until she found herself sitting on a pat of butter.

Although this story may seem very far removed from the IEP environment, there is in fact a great deal to be learned from it that is not only relevant but also extremely helpful.

On closer inspection, it is apparent that this very short story can be broken down into a series of developments, what could be called a *timeline,* that has five universal steps. These five steps can be called *universal* because they apply to everyone, everywhere, at every time in history. They are an integral part of the human condition and how we experience life. The timeline can help to clarify a great deal about emotions and about conflict, and it looks like this:

Event ⟶ Mental response ⟶ Feeling ⟶ Behavior ⟶ Consequence

In the IEP environment, a simple mnemonic makes it easier to remember these five universal steps: *Every Member Feels Better Collaboratively.*

If the two frogs were compared in terms of this five-point timeline, it would soon become evident that they first experienced an event and they both experienced the *same* event. What happened next, however, was very different for each of them.

They both fell into the milk, but the first frog was a pessimist. How can we know this? What was it about him that made him a pessimist? Whenever I ask this question in groups, I usually get several responses to the effect that he was a pessimist because he gave up. Yet if we look closely at the timeline, giving up is a behavior—an action—and it comes much later in the sequence of events. More accurately, he gave up because he was a pessimist and not the other way around. In fact, it is his *negative thinking* that characterizes and even defines his pessimism—his telling himself such things as there is no hope and there is no way out, both of which are mental responses, way upstream from the behavior of giving up that comes later in the series. The second frog was an optimist. We know this because of her positive mental responses, her positive thinking. She gave herself positive messages, such as "I know there's a way out" and "I know I can find it."

Moving on along the timeline, the next key element is feelings (emotions), and clearly the two frogs felt very differently, despite experiencing the very same event. The story does not tell us what they felt, but we can be pretty sure that the first frog felt negatively if he thought negatively and later gave up and sank. In fact, doesn't it always go together that if a person is thinking negatively, he or she is also feeling negatively? Has there ever been a pessimist who felt great?

So what negative emotions was the pessimistic frog most likely to be feeling? Perhaps he was feeling discouraged, despairing, or hopeless. In contrast, what was the optimistic frog likely to be feeling? She probably felt confident, determined, or hopeful. And what is it that led to their differing feelings if not their differing mental responses—their different ways of thinking!

Moving on down the timeline, the next category is behavior, and the question can be asked, "What did the two different frogs *do* with their different feelings?" Clearly the first frog gave up and sank, while the second kicked and splashed.

Finally, as a direct result of their differing behaviors, they encountered different consequences: the first frog drowned, while the second churned the milk into butter and survived. The story and the timeline are illustrated in the following chart.

	Event	Mental response	Feeling	Behavior	Consequence
Frog 1	Fell into Milk	Pessimism (negative thinking)	Hopeless	Gave up and sank	Drowned R.I.P.
Frog 2	Fell into Milk	Optimism (positive thinking)	Determined	Kicked and splashed	Churned milk into butter

The story of the frogs, while very simple, actually illustrates a number of very significant points:

1. Events don't shape feelings. Thinking does.

2. Thinking always leads to feelings.

3. Feelings are always expressed in some form of action.

4. Actions (behaviors) always have consequences.

It is worth taking a moment to consider just how significant these implications really are.

Partly because of culture and upbringing, most people seem to automatically accept that feelings are based on events. It is totally commonplace to say or hear such things as

I felt so upset because I wasn't invited to the party.

I was so nervous because the roads were icy this morning.

I was really angry because my boss gave the promotion to Sue.

On closer inspection of any of these statements, it becomes clear that they reflect a fundamental myth: They suggest that events determine feelings when there is always a critical intermediary. There is something absolutely decisive that fits between events and emotional response, and that is thinking (mental response)—whatever it is we are *telling ourselves* about the events that we encounter.

The universal timeline can be applied to any experience with the same essential truth being illustrated: It is not what happens to people in life but how they choose to look at it that determines how they feel, what they do, and what they encounter as a result. Table 4.1 shows alternatives in a person's silent, inner dialogue, what can be called *self-talk.* This fundamental principle—that thought determines feelings—is equally fitting in the IEP realm. Consider the variety of real-life possibilities from special education shown in Table 4.2.

Table 4.1.   Self-talk alternatives

Event	Mental response	Possible feeling	Possible behavior
Person loses a job	"I am such a failure."	Hopeless	Gives up
	"This will lead to something better."	Hopeful	Starts looking for another job
Person on a diet sees cake at a party	"Everyone else gets to eat some. Why not me?"	Cheated	Goes off the diet
	"They do what they want [eat] and so do I [diet]."	In control	Stays on the diet
Person is refused a date	"Nobody's interested in me."	Rejected	Stops asking for dates
	"That person is missing a golden opportunity."	Confident	Asks someone else
Person locks keys in car	"I'm so stupid!"	Foolish	Becomes tense and worries
	"Could happen to anyone."	Relaxed	Calmly seeks a solution
Person misses a deadline	"The boss will fire me!"	Fearful	Panics, hides, and frets
	"It's not the end of the world."	Assured	Confidently explains

Table 4.2. Self-talk alternatives at IEP meetings

Event	Mental response	Possible feeling	Possible behavior
Teacher is late for a meeting	"She doesn't care about anyone but herself."	Disrespected	Starts fuming
	"Maybe she had something important come up."	Concerned	Remains patient
Diagnostician is long-winded	"This guy just likes to hear himself talk."	Irritated	Confronts him abruptly
	"He means well and is trying his best to be helpful."	Appreciative	Gently refocuses him
Parent is angry at IEP suggestion	"She's really got a bad attitude."	Offended	Counterattacks
	"She doesn't yet realize our legal obligations."	Understanding	Asks for a moment to explain

Power Points

If the five-point timeline really does apply to all human experience and to the IEP environment as well, then where in the five-point timeline do people have the most power? Can people always control the events they encounter? No, certainly not. Can they control the way they think about them? Yes, absolutely: Mental response is definitely one of the greatest power points because whatever is happening in terms of events, people can always choose the way they want to think about them. This is illustrated in both the story of the frogs and the two self-talk charts: The way a person thinks will make a monumental difference.

Now, it must be emphasized that people can *not* always choose the thoughts that pop into their heads. What they can do, however, is choose the thoughts they want to entertain. Those that are negative, unproductive, or limiting they can simply ignore and replace with more positive alternatives. What a person is thinking is not just "the motor of the mind running on idle," like Ping-Pong balls bouncing around between the ears. Instead, thoughts are key elements in a creative process, and for that reason, all people can and *must* take control and no longer allow their mental responses to rule them by letting negative thinking lead them into negative feelings, negative actions, and then negative consequences.

It is also important to emphasize that not all thinking is conscious; in fact, most thinking is subconscious. That is, thoughts are usually without awareness until a person decides to be curious and begin to look for them. Equally worth noting is that most thinking is not in words! People usually think first in *imagery,* which is only later translated and expanded upon with words. A simple exercise will make this clear: If I ask you to think of your home for a moment, careful observation will invariably show that the first response is an image, soon followed with words ("Did I remember to lock the door? Better call about getting the windows cleaned. Wish they hadn't put that cell tower so close"). But whether in words or in images, the important implication is the same: Thinking is a major power point, and what anyone chooses to think will make all the difference in his or her life.

Are there any other power points? How about feelings? Can people control the way they *feel* about events? Many will quickly answer "yes," and yet it is not quite so simple. Feelings are not under immediate voluntary control. What this means is simply that people cannot change their feelings just by choosing to (as they can their thoughts). Most people have had someone tell them at some point, "You shouldn't feel that way" or "Don't feel like that." But was it helpful? Can a person suddenly stop feeling hurt or sad or angry just by choosing to? No, and this is because feelings are not under that immediate voluntary control. It is not that we, as human beings, have no power over our feelings or that we cannot change them once we feel bad. Rather, it is that the process of altering feelings requires more than simply choice. We have to work with them and know *how* to move them. More is said about this in a moment.

How about behavior? Is that another power point? Absolutely, and for the same reason as mental response: whatever is happening, people can choose what they will *do* about it. There is no such thing as doing nothing with feelings. Feelings are motivators, or animators, of behavior and will always be expressed in some form of action. Like the steam in an old-fashioned locomotive, they press for release and resolution. Allegedly doing nothing with feelings really means suppressing or avoiding them, or ruminating or muttering, or something similar, but certainly doing *something!* And that something always has consequences.

Consequences occur on three levels: for self (whether the person feels better as a result of the behavior), for other people (how the behavior is likely to affect them), and for the situation at hand (whether the event is somehow improved). What is very important to recognize is that it is the consequences of behavior that determine whether it can be called a good or bad way of expressing, releasing, and resolving the person's feelings.

Implications for Conflict

Once again, unpleasant feelings are a universal and *defining* feature of conflict. How a person expresses those feelings—that is, through behaviors—will be the single most decisive factor in determining where the conflict leads. Imagine that Mrs. Jones is a school administrator, and consider how much she can already know as soon as she hears that there is a conflict. Without a single detail as to the facts, she can safely assume a number of things. First, she can be sure that there are bad feelings involved. She also knows that those feelings reflect mental responses that follow some event that has happened, and she can be pretty sure those mental responses are negative. She also knows that the feelings people are experiencing are going to go somewhere. They don't exist in isolation and they *will* be expressed in action. And that action will always have consequences—for self, for others, and for the situation at hand. Most likely, the behaviors being chosen are not very productive or else she would not be hearing about the conflict because it would already be resolved!

The five-point timeline may be a new concept in some ways, and yet it is well understood by educators who are familiar with "the ABCs of the FBA," that is, with looking for the antecedents, behaviors, and consequences (ABCs) whenever they do what is called a functional behavior analysis (FBA). The focus, when it comes to antecedents, however, has usually been only on events—what is happening before the child shows the particular behavior being observed. It is time to add mental responses and feelings to the FBA model, which has so much in common with the five-point timeline. In other words, one can begin to question what the child is thinking and feeling between the events and the target behavior.

The second half of the timeline includes the feeling-behavior-consequence segments. Indeed, "every member feels better collaboratively." The second half of the sequence is even more decisive than the first because what is even more critical than what people think and feel is what they choose to *do* with it.

BEHAVIOR TRAINS

Having examined where feelings come from (mental responses to events), let's focus now on *where they go*—how they are expressed in behavior. *Behavior trains* are a helpful means of illustrating this inevitable process of expression. Behavior trains were made popular decades ago by the school of thought known as behavioral psychology. They are a means of mapping out the various alternatives available for the expression of any one feeling and for comparing the behavioral options in terms of their consequences. A behavior train diagram, once completed, looks similar to a railroad map, with each of the behavioral choices leading off in different directions. The basic premise is that, given any one feeling, there will be a wide variety of behaviors with which a person might express that one feeling, and the way to decide which is a good or a bad way to express it is by looking at the consequences.

Behavior Trains Illustrated

Imagine that 15-year-old Sam feels hurt at his IEP meeting. There must have been a precipitating event (something happened), and he must have done some negative thinking about that event (whether consciously or not, accurately or not, and in words or in images). For the sake of illustration, let's assume that he feels hurt because he believes that no one cares what he thinks, after the team rejects his proposal that the school provide funding for his summer football camp. The consensus of the team is that this is not related to his IEP needs and therefore not something they can either approve or fund.

Let's start with Sam's feelings of hurt. If he feels this way, what might be some of the behaviors with which he will express it? Perhaps he will assume a "long face," slump down in his chair, and mutter quietly to himself. Or maybe he will get angry and lash out with name-calling or even swearing, or stomp out of the room and slam the door behind him. Maybe he will keep his feelings to himself and later go for a walk, mow the lawn, or practice throwing a basketball. There is really no such thing as doing nothing, so if he is seemingly doing nothing, he might be denying, avoiding, or suppressing. Obviously there are a great many ways in which he might express his hurt feelings, but they will certainly motivate him into *some* form of action. These different possibilities can be charted as a behavior train, which appears on the following page.

Consequences of Behavior

Each of these behaviors in the illustration can be evaluated in terms of their positive or negative consequences for self, others, and situation, as indicated by the checkmarks and Xs following each one. What soon becomes apparent is that *most* of Sam's behavioral choices will help him feel better, some will be acceptable to others, but not one of them will address the situation that he feels troubled about— the refusal of the team to fund his summer football camp (and his belief that they don't really care what he thinks).

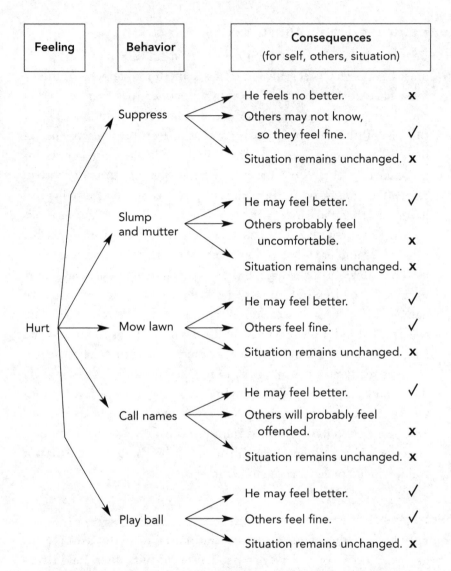

Feeling	Behavior	Consequences (for self, others, situation)	
	Suppress	He feels no better.	**x**
		Others may not know, so they feel fine.	✓
		Situation remains unchanged.	**x**
	Slump and mutter	He may feel better.	✓
		Others probably feel uncomfortable.	**x**
		Situation remains unchanged.	**x**
Hurt	Mow lawn	He may feel better.	✓
		Others feel fine.	✓
		Situation remains unchanged.	**x**
	Call names	He may feel better.	✓
		Others will probably feel offended.	**x**
		Situation remains unchanged.	**x**
	Play ball	He may feel better.	✓
		Others feel fine.	✓
		Situation remains unchanged.	**x**

Of course, there are many more possible behaviors he could choose, but there is a good chance they will also fail the three-point test, especially the final one of whether the behaviors will meaningfully address the situation (event) that the feelings relate to. It can be very helpful to understand that it is precisely because so many of these behaviors *do* help people feel better that they keep them! They are what psychologists call functional. It begins to make sense now why so many people do so many "goofy" things to cope with and express their feelings. Different people may choose different behaviors: One may escape by getting drunk while another gets lost in his work; one may quietly watch television while another explodes in rage. Yet all of these various behaviors help people feel better, if only in the short term and despite their many limitations in terms of how others are likely to respond and whether the circumstances are improved. With this in mind, the following wonderful saying comes to have great meaning:

However obnoxious someone is on the surface, underneath that somewhere he or she is hurting, and underneath *that* is a worthwhile person.

Good Behavioral Alternatives

What behavioral choices are there that can be considered good ones? What *can* people do with their feelings to ensure a positive outcome in terms of the three criteria (self, others, and situation)? The answer is simple, though not commonly understood, and that is *effective communication*. Effective communication is the only behavior that has a strong likelihood of ensuring a positive outcome—at least insofar as possible. This qualifier must be added because one can never really guarantee how other people will respond. (They, too, have their own thoughts, feelings, and behavioral choices.) Yet with effective communication, Sam (the student in this example) has the very best chance of a behavior train with positive consequences on all three levels, and one that looks something like this:

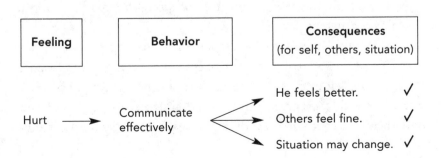

Will the IEP team fund his football camp if he communicates effectively? Well, that depends on whether he can persuade them that his request is truly relevant to his IEP. Let's assume for present purposes that the answer remains "no." As they begin to communicate about the situation, Sam can have a chance to speak and be heard, clear the air, and thus resolve his unpleasant feelings. Furthermore, through productive discussion, he may come into a new understanding that will lead him to a different, more accurate, and *more positive* mental response to the same event (of no funding for camp). This process of effective communication can also lead him to change his thinking that the others don't really care. In a sense, he will move from being a pessimistic frog to being an optimistic frog and thus, predictably, into new and more positive feelings that replace his feelings of hurt. It is also possible that, by communicating together, the team may come up with *another* plan so that everyone can, through collaboration leading to consensus, walk away feeling comfortable with the decision they have made together. As an example, perhaps they will all agree to help Sam try out for any of the school's athletic teams but not to fund a summer football camp.

RESOLVING BAD FEELINGS

As explained earlier, feelings are not one of the power points on the five-point timeline because, unlike mental responses and behaviors, they cannot be changed simply by choice. The example of Sam's IEP meeting, however, gives insights into how we *can* change our feelings, though the process is not quite as straightforward as simply choosing a different one.

A helpful analogy to the movement of feelings is a nice, hot bath. If a person is sitting in a tub of cold and dirty water and wants to take a hot, clean bath, the best solution is not to simply add hot water. Instead, the person must first drain the existing water and only then replace it with new (hot and clean) water. Similarly, if anyone feels badly as a result of negative thinking, it is not enough to simply layer those bad feelings with positive thoughts and feelings. That is, the person must do more than simply add positives on top of the negatives because the negatives would then remain very much alive underneath. Instead, it is necessary to first "drain the tub," and this is where effective communications can be so valuable.

As described in the previous example, Sam drains his tub when he acknowledges how he feels. By talking about his hurt feelings, he gets them off his chest. So much for letting out the cold, dirty water. But the second part is equally important: He changes the way he thinks as a result of the understanding that comes from productive discussion, and his new and more positive thinking is what puts the hot, clean water in his tub.

This analogy of water to emotions is something that is presented again in discussing the search for serenity in Chapter 6. For now, consider how frequently the word *effective* has been used with regard to dialogue, discussion, and communication. It is time to look now at just what constitutes effective communication.

KEYS TO EFFECTIVE COMMUNICATION

Without doubt, effective communication skills are of critical importance in nearly all aspects of successful living and for a number of reasons, including clarifying thoughts and interests, resolving bad feelings, and helping to restore collaboration and team spirit. But what exactly constitutes effective communication? If I feel hurt and I start giving everyone the silent treatment or if I yell and slam doors, aren't I communicating? Certainly! But is this effective communication? Certainly not.

From many years of studying and facilitating communication between people, first as a counselor and later as a mediator, I have come to see four key aspects to effective communication. Like the four tires on a car, all of them are important. These four keys are

---

Keys to Effective Communication

1. **Hold a focus** (let one person speak at a time and about only one topic at a time)

2. **Talk from the heart** (clearly express feelings and wants)

3. **Listen with respect** (listen like a sponge)

4. **Maintain the spirit of friendship**

Hold a Focus

In observing people as they discuss an issue, it can often be seen that they quickly move into so many topics at once that nothing gets resolved and no one really feels heard. As an example,

Jill: I'm really angry that you never sent me a copy of the test results before this meeting.

Mark: Well, I've had a million things to do these last few weeks, and I can't be expected to remember everything.

Jill: But I am entitled to receive copies.

Mark: Excuse me, but if this was really important to you, you could have called to remind me.

While it may be absolutely true that Mark had many things to do recently and that Jill could have taken some responsibility for obtaining the test report, Mark's responses do not hold a focus on *her* issues or *her* feelings. Instead, they promptly shift the focus back to his. The result is likely to be an escalation of accusations, defenses, and bad feelings on both parts without any productive resolution. Even worse, Jill may conclude that when she has a concern, talking to Mark is useless. If this happens, their communications will break down and with that may go any power they have to resolve disagreements and bad feelings in the future.

Holding a focus simply involves taking turns in expressing feelings, wants, and dissatisfactions. It is a matter of *timing* and not a matter of who is right or wrong or whose thoughts and feelings are of greater or lesser importance. Once the person who has the floor first has had a chance to speak and be heard, it may then be the appropriate time to "move the spotlight" and give the other person an opportunity to respond. When that appropriate juncture arrives, the best way to shift the focus to the other person's thoughts and feelings is *by asking!*

Returning to the test report example, if Mark wanted to hold a focus, he might respond to Jill as follows:

Jill: I'm really angry that you never sent me a copy of the test results before this meeting.

Mark: Say some more about that.

Jill: I am entitled to see them, and nobody sent them to me, so I have no idea what Mary's reading level even is.

Mark: So you wanted the results so as to be sure what her present levels are before the meeting, right?

Jill: Yes. How can we develop an IEP if we don't know how she's doing?

Mark: I see what you mean. May I respond to what you've said?

Mark has not agreed that Jill is right (although perhaps she is), but he is holding a focus on her thoughts and feelings and not shifting that focus until given permission to do so. This allows Jill to express herself and be heard, and it shows her that Mark is open to hearing what she has to say. By Mark's asking for permission before he responds, Jill is much more likely to be open and listening when he gives his side of the story. His side might be "I'm really sorry. I meant to but somehow forgot" or instead "Yes, you definitely have a right to see the test results, but it is up to you to take the initiative to ask for them." The key here is, again, not who is right or wrong but the timing of their dialogue. Their communication will be much more productive if a focus is held—one person and one topic at a time.

Talk from the Heart

By definition, to *talk from the heart* means to clearly identify two important things: what you feel and what you want—right here and right now. Some people confuse talking from the heart with being sincere; although sincerity is always important, it is the clear expression of feelings and wishes that make it what it is.

Most people are comfortable with expressing what they think but much less comfortable with sharing what they really feel. And although people may talk at great length about whatever it is that is bothering them, they are often extremely vague about what it is they want! The importance of these two simple points cannot be overstated: there is a significant power that comes with the direct expression of *feelings,* and there is a tremendous potential for success that can often come only with the clear expression of what the person is asking for—not in general but right here and now.

Compare the alternatives in the following scenarios:

Mom 1:   I am really sick of hearing that I'm not doing enough.

Mom 2:   I **feel really discounted** when you tell me he needs more assistance at home. I spend a lot of time with him and **want you to recognize** the efforts my husband and I are making.

Chair 1:   This unprofessionalism has to stop. It's time we all start doing what we were hired to do.

Chair 2:   I **feel very concerned** about the time we lose when people leave in the middle of our meetings. I'd like each of us to **take steps** to see that our meetings don't get interrupted.

Teacher 1: These new policies are just ridiculous. Somebody needs to cut us a little slack around here.

Teacher 2: I am **feeling really overwhelmed** lately. I **want your understanding** that this meeting is not my only obligation.

Notice that the issue of talking from the heart is, again, not a matter of right and wrong or of should and shouldn't. It is a means of clear and direct communication that serves a variety of important purposes:

- Clearing the air (feelings begin to resolve when they are acknowledged)

- Commanding respect (there is power in the direct expression of feelings)

- Raising awareness by clarifying thoughts, feelings, goals, and interests

- Providing an opportunity to receive support and assistance

A fundamental principle to consider is to "ask for what you want." So often when an interaction with others is not successful or productive, it is blamed on the other people being unreasonable or uncaring. Most of the time, however, it is really more a matter of well-intentioned people getting caught up in miscommunications and misunderstandings.

Listen with Respect

To *listen with respect* is to listen like a sponge. Too often, people are so busy formulating their own responses or defenses when they listen that they may not really be listening at all. To listen does not necessarily mean to agree. It only communicates that the listener cares about, respects, values, includes, and is open to the person who is speaking. Conversely, to *not* listen effectively communicates a long list of the opposite: not respecting, not valuing, being closed minded, and so on. If what a person *does* communicate is that he or she is not really listening, how likely will others be to feel included and respected and to talk openly with that person in the future?

When the other person has the floor, the listener can make a point to offer the same attention and respect that will be appreciated when the listener's turn to speak arrives. A simple test for listeners is this: At any point in the conversation, can they repeat back to the speaker the essence of what the speaker is saying to them? Each party has valid perspectives and feelings. Most people have room to grow in this seemingly simple area.

Maintain the Spirit of Friendship

In considering some of the typical communication styles that surface during meetings, there are certain styles that usually promote success and others that, instead, tend to promote tension and discord. Some people communicate competitively (trying to convince or coerce others to their own points of view). A few may communicate combatively (with hostility, blame, and attack). It is not so much what they say as the way they say it. An important quality is missing, one that could perhaps be called *the spirit of friendship.* Some people communicate sheepishly, almost in whines and whimpers, showing no respect (friendship) to themselves!

Whether the speaker likes the other person or not, whether he or she agrees with the other person or not, the speaker can always choose to say whatever it might be with the spirit of respect and friendship. There is very little which cannot be expressed with this quality when a person recognizes its importance and simply wants to. When you think back to conversations in your own experience that didn't work out well, was it a matter of what was said or *how* it was said? And was it the person, per se, or the *attitude* the person seemed to show? So often, it is just that key ingredient of the spirit of friendship that was missing, and it all went downhill from there. But it might have worked out very differently if that one key ingredient had been present.

Once it is accepted that the spirit of friendship is vitally important for productive communication, all a person usually needs next is just what I call "the great big W" of willingness. When a person simply *wants* to communicate with friendship and respect, holding that intention clearly in mind, whatever is said next will usually reflect that positive intention.

Communication is indeed the very key to effective teams and to successful relationships in any setting. With effective communication skills, nearly all differences can be worked through and successfully resolved. Conversely, with faulty communication skills, the most minor of differences can become insurmountable, leading to major conflict and a host of harmful side effects. A helpful question to ask whenever problems are encountered that do not seem to get resolved is this:

> *Have I clearly and directly expressed what I feel and what I want with self-respect in the spirit of friendship?*

Most of the time that problems are ongoing, the answer is *no*—the person has not yet communicated quite so clearly or directly with that all-important spirit. The good news, then, is that there is still hope, there is more that can be done, and the person still has power!

NOTES ABOUT ANGER

One of the most familiar emotions, of course, is anger. Curiously, anger is also one of the emotions that many people are most comfortable talking about when it comes to telling others "exactly how they feel," a phrase that is usually associated with critical, angry comments. However, anger stands in a very special category all its own. By referring back to the five-point timeline and behavior trains, it soon becomes apparent why this is so.

A few options for the expression of the feeling of hurt were mapped out earlier in exploring the options for Sam, the student who is unhappy when his IEP team refuses to fund his summer football camp. One of the alternatives presented was that Sam could get angry, and perhaps stomp out of the room or lash out and call names. In other words, one possible behavior train he can follow when he feels hurt is to get angry. This can be illustrated as follows:

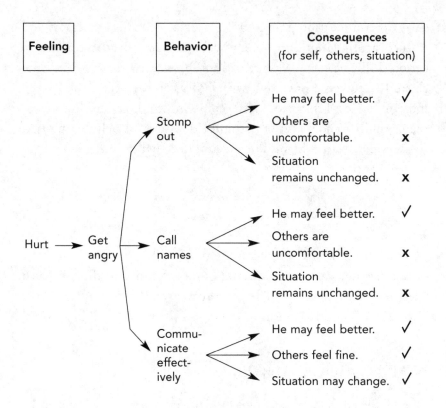

Note that there is an additional section to the railroad track in this example. Instead of only one category between feeling and consequences, as in all of the earlier examples, there are now two. While it is clear enough that stomping out, calling names, or communicating effectively are behaviors, where does anger fit best? Is it a behavior or is it a feeling? Well, in some ways, it is *both*.

Anger is best viewed as a *secondary emotion,* meaning a feeling that follows something else that a person feels first. In this regard, it differs from so many other feelings that might precede or underlie it. Yes, anger is a feeling, but it is also a coping response, and for that reason it is also, in a real sense, a behavior. However, because it will also motivate its own behavioral expression, it is not a behavior in quite the same way that other behaviors are. In the example above, hurt is clearly the primary feeling, anger may be considered a secondary feeling, and any of the three actions—stomping, name-calling, or communicating—are behavioral alternatives that might express the anger, each leading to its own consequences.

Implications of Anger as Secondary

Is this purely an intellectual exercise or does it have practical value? Well, it definitely does have value. Imagine that a friend is confronting Jane about neglecting to invite him to her party. If he stays with his primary feeling of hurt, for example, he may say, "I really felt hurt when I wasn't invited to your party." If instead he chooses to become angry, he may say, "I'm so mad at you for not sending me an invitation." Which would probably sit better with Jane? Is she likely to think, feel, and respond differently? Almost certainly the answer will be *yes*.

Anger almost always has a distancing effect between people, while the more primary emotions *tend* to inspire a response of concern and compassion. It is important to qualify and say "tend" because there are no guarantees as to how any particular person will think or feel in any given situation. It is therefore necessary to speak in generalizations, although they are usually fairly safe bets.

Because as the saying goes, "you get back what you send out," the expression of anger will usually invite defensiveness and perhaps a counterattack in return. The typical consequences of the choice to become angry, rather than staying with the primary feelings underneath it, include

1. Promoting distance with others

2. Promoting negative feelings in others

3. Inviting retaliation and/or defensiveness

4. Masking the underlying feelings and thoughts

5. Hindering productive problem solving

That's a good list of reasons to stay with the primary feelings!

The Four Pillars

There are four feelings that *usually* precede anger, and these include fear, hurt, frustration, and injustice. Although the list of possible underlying feelings may be much longer, these four are probably the most common and could be called "the four pillars that hold up the roof of anger." Whenever someone is angry (even if it is our own selves), these four are a good place to look first.

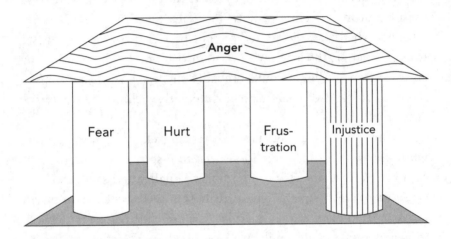

As with all feelings, anger also follows mental responses. Thus, to feel angry *because* of anything (events) can be misleading; the mental responses (thoughts) behind the anger must also be considered. A few alternatives can be compared in which anger is the consistent and most apparent feature, and yet any of a variety of thoughts and primary feelings may underlie it. As illustrated in Table 4.3, the possible thoughts and underlying feelings may differ greatly and yet result in the same one feeling of anger.

As mentioned before, anger frequently reflects fear, hurt, frustration, or a sense of injustice, but the list of possible underlying feelings is by no means limited to these four. Although they are a good place to begin to look, there are a great many possible underlying feelings, which are summarized in the following chart.

Table 4.3. Possible antecedents of anger

Event	Mental response	Primary feeling	Behavior
Teacher is late.	"We won't have enough time to complete the IEP today."	Fear	Becomes angry
	"She is so inconsiderate!"	Injustice	Becomes angry
	"She wouldn't be late if she *liked* Johnny."	Hurt	Becomes angry
	"Every time we meet, we are always so rushed."	Frustration	Becomes angry

Feelings that Typically Underlie Anger

Abandoned	Exhausted	Ignored	Overwhelmed
Anxious	Fearful	Imposed upon	Persecuted
Ashamed	Foolish	Inadequate	Pressured
Attacked	Frantic	Injustice	Put down
Betrayed	Frustration	Intimidated	Rejected
Burdened	Grief	Isolated	Sad
Cheated	Guilty	Jealous	Threatened
Criticized	Helpless	Left out	Trapped
Defeated	Hopeless	Lonely	Vulnerable
Dominated	Hurt	Nervous	Worried

To emphasize that anger is a secondary emotion is not to say that it is bad or that a person should never feel that way. Instead, it is only to encourage teams to look beyond the surface and be curious about the thoughts and feelings that lie beneath it. Such openness, paired with effective communication in the spirit of friendship, can help to resolve bad feelings and restore a spirit of togetherness. In so doing, teams can make lemonade from any lemons and get back on track to working collaboratively toward consensus for the benefit of the children (and all involved).

Chapter 5

Diplomacy and Support of Feelings

THE SULTAN AND HIS WISE MEN

A great sultan called on his three wise men to predict his future. The first said, "Oh, great master, I see a terrible future ahead for you. You will lose all your loved ones and die an old, bitter, and very lonely man." The sultan was horrified by the story he heard, and he banished this man from his kingdom.

He then called his second wise man, who said, "Master, I see that you will bury all those you love and hold dear." The sultan was horrified by this vision as well. He became enraged and ordered this wise man to leave the palace and never return.

He then called the third and last of his wise men, who said, "Great master, I see that you will live a very long and healthy life." Upon hearing this, the sultan was so much relieved that he gave him a handsome reward.

It is usually easy to recognize the importance of diplomacy. Most people would readily agree that it is often more a matter of *how* something is said, rather than *what* is being said, when it comes to promoting or avoiding conflict. Yet there can be a big difference between recognizing a truth and being skilled at expressing that truth; people often understand diplomacy far better than they can do it!

Because diplomacy is so important for successfully working with others, it warrants a chapter all its own. It is indeed a skill every team member can put to good use, and it very much supports the keys to effective communication covered in the previous chapter, especially with regard to promoting a spirit of respect and friendship. This chapter will cover four aspects of diplomacy and then focus on how to show support of feelings—something very often needed when working in the IEP environment.

FOUR ASPECTS OF DIPLOMACY

A helpful way of approaching the broad topic of diplomacy is to explore it from the following perspectives:

1. Communicating so as to be well-received by the listener

2. Responding, as opposed to keeping silent

3. Saying "no" in a way that preserves a positive relationship

4. Knowing what to say when you don't know what to say

Certainly the last three are subsets of the first, in that response versus silence, saying "no," and knowing what to say when you don't know what to say are all aspects of communicating so as to be well-received. Yet these last three are not only less obvious features of diplomacy, they are also areas where the potential for conflict is increased. All of these aspects of diplomacy surface in the IEP environment, just as they do in so many areas of interpersonal relationships, and so each warrants careful consideration.

From Well-Meant to Well-Said

As a training exercise, I will sometimes present a group with a list of true statements, all of which may be very well-intentioned and yet clearly too direct and insensitive, or even blunt, for anyone to recommend them as being the best ways to express the thoughts a person might want to communicate. And so the group is then asked to, in a sense, translate these statements from well-meant to well-said. The fun begins from there!

A few examples will help clarify the ingredients that offer the greatest chance of success, as well as those more likely to promote discord. Let's take as a basic assumption that every one of the following statements is absolutely true. Instead of their validity, let's just focus on the wisdom of phrasing the truth in such direct terms. While some may think of themselves as just too honest, it is rarely their honesty that gets them into trouble. A ditty to consider is that "truth without kindness can be devastating."

EXAMPLE 1: YOU'RE NOT ALONE. A LOT OF PEOPLE HAVE CHILDREN WITH SPECIAL NEEDS.

Yes, approximately 12% of the public school population has been designated as having special educational needs. Yet to equate the individual's emotional experience with that of a group can easily be seen as minimizing, or even trivializing, and certainly not respecting the feelings that the individual may have. In addition, it may be seen as judging the person as being somehow inappropriate in holding the feelings that he or she does (and anything suggesting that "you shouldn't feel that way" is only likely to add shame, insecurity, and negative reactions to whatever other feelings are already present). Instead, it may be best to avoid comparisons, simply respect people to feel as they do, and encourage them to express and share their feelings, perhaps by saying something like, "This can be hard for some people. How are you doing with it?" The lessons that can be taken from this example include that people *should* feel however they do and that teams can make it okay by affirming that a particular situation may be hard for some people.

EXAMPLE 2: YOU ONLY FEEL BAD BECAUSE YOU BELIEVE WE DON'T CARE.

Once again, this may be absolutely true—when people believe that others don't care about them or their feelings or their children, they probably feel any number of negative feelings. And if they believe it, *even when it is not true,* they will probably still feel those same bad feelings. At the same time, what are the likely repercussions of confronting people in such terms? Aren't they likely to feel belittled or rejected and certainly not supported, valued, included, or safe? Instead, teams can encourage their members to feel welcome to share their thoughts and feelings, knowing that acknowledging feelings helps to move and resolve them, and that owning negative thinking often leads to its reassessment and revision. Thus, asking a person, "Have I said something that upsets you?" might open the door for such clarification and expression without pointing fingers in any way. This question incorporates two valuable techniques that will be presented again in a later chapter: checking it out and pointing at self. Yet another helpful approach might be to simply share the good intention, "Mr. Doe, I really want to be on your side," and then perhaps talk from the heart (feelings and wants): "My fear is that you see me as uncaring, and I really want to fix that if it's true."

EXAMPLE 3: WE'VE ALL FELT GRIEF BEFORE, TOO.

This, of course, is a variation on "you're not alone" (the first example) in that it also categorizes the individual with the group. Certainly we *have* all felt grief before, but there is always a risk that the person hearing this will see it as trivializing rather than affirming the individual's experience, which may serve to block rather than encourage further self-expression. Instead "How are you doing with that?" or "Would you like to set a time to talk about this together?" may promote a perception of interest, caring, and safety.

Example 4: You're Being Totally Unreasonable and Not Listening to Anything We Say.

If it is true that the person is not listening, why might that be? Is the team member feeling attacked? Has something been said that leads the person to feel a need to pull back and defend? Does the member feel powerless and controlled? Is the person generalizing from *some other* bad experience? Maybe what is most needed here is to yield the floor and provide an opportunity for the "totally unreasonable" person to speak and be heard. "Diffusing to the group" by making a general statement may be more effective than confronting the individual, as in "Team, I am wondering if we are all having a chance to speak and be heard. Maybe it would be helpful if we each had a chance to say what we think. Mr. Doe, what are your thoughts?" Doing so can help to accomplish several important things: to encourage the clarification and verbalizing of thoughts, encourage productive expression of feelings, and avoid pointing fingers at any one member of the team.

Example 5: Anger Is a Secondary Emotion. What Are You *Really* Feeling?

It is certainly true that anger always follows something else, something closer to the heart, that someone is feeling first (perhaps hurt, fear, frustration, or injustice). Yet to ask "What are you *really* feeling?" is to suggest that he or she is not really feeling anger, which is only likely to fan the fires into some more *very real* anger! Also, to publicly confront a person with not sharing underlying feelings may be perceived as critical and embarrassing. Generally speaking, most people are not highly aware of their feelings, and few feel safe enough to share them in a group even when they are aware. So in this example, the speaker can lift the lid on the pressure cooker by encouraging the person to express his or her feelings in whatever way feels most comfortable for the particular person. One option is to say something like "Mr. Doe, I sense this issue is important to you. Can you tell us more about it?"

EXAMPLE 6: YOU'RE INTERRUPTING ME AND RAISING YOUR VOICE AGAIN.

This is an example of an intervention technique called *confronting the individual*. It certainly has its place, but very often a softer touch would be more effective and safer. It is usually best to avoid the likelihood that the person will feel humiliated or belittled, especially in front of the group, and the same objectives can often be achieved in a more effective way. And what are those objectives, if not that all members of the group will feel free to share openly in a respectful environment, that all will abide by the agreed-upon ground rules (such as avoiding hostility and name calling), and that the team will accomplish whatever is on its agenda for the day. Instead of confronting, the speaker can share the good intention by saying, "Mr. Doe, I really want to hear your thoughts about this." And then, after Mr. Doe has had a chance to speak and be heard, the speaker can ask for permission to shift focus: "May I respond to what you have said?" If interruptions and raised voices continue, a different approach may be necessary—perhaps reminding Mr. Doe of the ground rules. (Hopefully, they *were* set at the beginning of the meeting.) Such a reminder can be done in the most respectful terms possible, perhaps in saying to the group as a whole, without even looking at Mr. Doe:

> Team, I am feeling a little uncomfortable right now. I am remembering our agreement not to interrupt and raise voices. I really want to hear everyone's thoughts. I also would like a chance to respond, and I'm sure you all would, too. Does that sound fair to everyone?

A long list of statements that might be made at IEP meetings could be presented, but perhaps this is not necessary. Below is a general summary of things to do and things to avoid. Some additional alternatives will be provided later in this book when specific intervention options are covered.

Do	Want to be supportive, understanding, and encouraging (the big W of willingness)
	Provide a climate of safety to feel and think however participants do
	Look for underlying feelings and encourage their acknowledgment
	Respect feelings and thoughts at all times, even when your own are different
	Encourage clarification of thoughts so they can be owned and reassessed
	Use the softest possible touch and the least necessary force
	Remember that truth without kindness can have very sharp edges
Avoid	Minimizing or generalizing the individual's experience
	Pointing fingers at anyone other than self (use "I" terms)
	Confronting or embarrassing anyone in front of the group
	Pressing members to talk beyond their comfort zones

The Importance of Response

People are busy, no doubt about that. And people are often focused on their own immediate concerns, trying hard to do their best, perhaps under very challenging circumstances. As a result, what happens all too often is that other people, their issues, and their feelings may be overlooked or forgotten. Messages are sometimes not relayed, calls may not be returned, questions may not be answered, and tasks may not be completed. Of course, very often, these messages, questions, and tasks *are* in motion and will be taken care of. They are not really lost, merely delayed amid the long list of responsibilities so many people carry. And now comes the "but."

What are the implications for harmony or discord when people get so busy that they neglect to respond to one another in a timely and professional manner? How does Mr. Jones feel when he calls the school, leaves a message, and gets no reply? How does Mrs. Smith feel when she sends a letter or an e-mail that remains unanswered? Silence generally leaves a void, and most people are inclined to fill such voids with fantasies. That is, when they have nothing to go by, they tend to be creative and fill the gaps in their understanding based on their past experience. They may supplement that experience with their own perceptions and expectations, their fears and assumptions, and any rumors or gossip they may have heard from others. All things being equal, people generally tend to paint pictures more negatively than perhaps they should. However, in the IEP environment, things are not always equal—often the lack of response a person receives comes on the heels of years of experience that has not always been pleasant. Negative interpretations of silence can contribute greatly to the very things teams want to *avoid* in the IEP environment: suspicion, mistrust, anger, and conflict. It is important, therefore, to recognize the extreme value of *response,* as opposed to silence, and to consider how very helpful the alternatives can be—how valuable just a few minutes of time and attention can be in promoting trust and respect and maintaining good will and cooperation.

A few recommendations in this regard: Team members can make notes on their calendars when friendly reminders, touching base, or following up might be a good idea. A simple call or e-mail to say that you are looking into it and have not forgotten the question or issue can pay big dividends in team spirit and conflict prevention. If a team member is too busy to do so personally, perhaps an assistant or coworker can be asked to help: "Mary, would you mind calling Mr. Smith and letting him know we got his message and are looking into the matter?" If there is no news, a simple note to that effect can be very reassuring: "Mrs. Green, just wanted to let you know we are still waiting for the test results we spoke about. I don't have any news but did want you to know I hadn't forgotten." People rarely, if ever, get into trouble for being too concerned, too respectful, or too helpful. It can therefore be very worthwhile to stay aware of who is asking or waiting for what, and how best to keep them informed and show that you care.

Saying "No"

Saying "no" when appropriate is a skill that all people *must* have in the toolbox of life. At the same time, saying "no" inherently means that a person is not giving someone whatever it is he or she is asking for. For obvious reasons, therefore, this topic provides an elevated need for diplomacy, and the ability to say "no" without losing friends can sometimes be a challenging task. How can we say "no" without someone feeling offended? How can we preserve mutual respect and team spirit when at the same denying others what it is they say they want? As with all aspects of diplomacy, the probability of success or failure will depend very much on *how* we say "no," far more so than *whether* we say "no," and so it is worth examining this issue in some detail.

There are four key elements to consider when saying "no," and including them *all* will usually provide the best chance of preserving good will and assuring a favorable response. These four are

---

Keys to Saying No

1. Providing an explanation
2. Offering an alternative
3. Showing support for the other person's position
4. Inviting the other person's response

Imagine that Mrs. Adams is asking that her son, John, be moved to a different school where she feels certain he will have a greater chance of success. Let's examine some alternatives in the way a person might reply, and see how each of the four keys could make a difference in the probable outcome.

Example 1

I'm sorry, but that really is not an option at this time.

If this is the response she receives, is there any hope that Mrs. Adams will feel good about it or remain a cheerful and fully involved member of the team? Very unlikely. Note that this sample response includes none of the four keys that were listed above.

Example 2

I'm sorry, Mrs. Adams, but we really can't do that. The district policy is that we cannot move children to a different school unless it has been clearly established that their educational needs can not be met where they are currently placed.

How about this one? Is there a greater chance that this explanation will be well received, and that team spirit and positive relationships will be preserved? Well, possibly. After all, the speaker certainly did provide an explanation, which is one of the four keys. But one key out of four leaves lots of room for improvement. Let's look at some other options and see if they might work any better.

Example 3

I'm sorry, Mrs. Adams, but we really can't do that unless John's educational needs cannot be met at his present school. What we *can* do is a careful review of his progress, and see whether his needs could be met here, and then perhaps consider the possibility of moving him.

This third example not only provides an explanation but also proposes an alternative, one that may address the parent's concerns. This example includes two out of four of the features that make for success and probably raises the chance of a favorable reception, but there may still be room for improvement. The next example includes three keys—it adds the element of showing support, simply by acknowledging what the parent might be thinking or feeling:

Example 4

I'm sorry, Mrs. Adams, but we really can't do that unless John's educational needs cannot be met at his present school. What we *can* do is a careful review of his progress, and see whether his needs could be met here, and then perhaps consider the possibility of moving him. I can imagine that this might seem long way around the mountain and even very frustrating for you.

As a final example, and one that incorporates *all* of the keys, the following adds the fourth key ingredient of inviting a response:

Example 5

I'm sorry, Mrs. Adams, but we really can't do that unless John's educational needs cannot be met at his present school. What if we do a careful review of his progress, and see whether his needs could be met here, and then perhaps consider the possibility of moving him? I know this might seem like a waste of time and be very frustrating for you. Even so, how would that sound as a possibility?

Notice that the alternative of reviewing John's progress is phrased not as a statement but *as a question* (asking is affirming). Inviting the parent's response is further enhanced by specifically asking how the proposal sounds to her. By asking such questions with sincere caring and true openness, it is amazing how often team spirit can be maintained and perhaps even strengthened, even when saying "no." Would you disagree?

When You Don't Know What to Say

Another type of challenge arises when someone really doesn't know *what* to say. Perhaps the person feels stuck or at a loss for words. Or maybe the person feels uncertain or intimidated. Perhaps he or she doesn't yet know the answer to whatever question or issue is at hand. In any of a variety of possible situations, team members benefit from knowing what they *can* say when they really don't know what to say.

As mentioned earlier, saying or doing nothing can leave some uncomfortable spaces that will often be filled with negative assumptions. Because there really is no such thing as doing nothing, when people are keeping silent because they don't know what to say, then most likely what they *really are* doing is suppressing their feelings and trying to avoid dealing with the situation.

Most people who don't know what to say are feeling uncomfortable and some form of anxiety. A helpful alternative at such a time is a process known as sharing the conflict. Instead of avoiding or keeping quiet, team members can simply talk from the heart by sharing what they feel and what they want in the immediate moment that they don't know what to say.

If, for example, the IEP team seems to be losing a focus and wandering in different directions, I might find myself feeling irritated but I'm not sure what to say. I could share my conflict by saying, "Team, I feel a little nervous about the time, and I'd like some help staying on track." Note that this is simply talking from the heart with a clear expression of feelings and wishes. (I feel nervous and want help staying on track.) Note also that, in the interests of diplomacy, I might rephrase my feeling irritated (a mild form of anger) by expressing the underlying feeling (nervous) and softening my words by adding "a little" to my expression of nervousness.

As a second example, perhaps Mr. Brown is raising his voice and I find myself feeling intimidated but I'm not sure what to say. I could share the conflict by saying, "Mr. Brown, I am feeling a little intimidated right now. I'm interested in your thoughts and wonder if you can speak a little softer?" Again, I can be careful in selecting words that will achieve my objective (of a more cooperative tone from Mr. Brown) without coming across as critical or offensive. Note also the use of "and" as opposed to "but" when saying, "I am interested in your thoughts *and* wonder. . . ."

What about those situations that aren't quite so clear—when people not only don't know what to say but aren't sure what they are feeling or what they want? These can be times when sharing the conflict is *not* just a matter of talking from the heart. Imagine that I am feeling uncomfortable but don't know for sure what exactly I am feeling, and whether it is fear, hurt, anger, intimidation, or some other emotion. Such feeling labels as *concerned, uncertain,* and *uncomfortable* are relatively safe blanket words that can cover (and even mask) a great many more precise feeling words. They tend to be less pointed and less confrontational than some of the more accurate labels that might otherwise be used, especially if qualified by "a little bit" or "somewhat" concerned, uncertain, and so on. Thus, whether team members even know what they are feeling, for purposes of sharing the conflict, they can always begin with "I am feeling a little concerned" or something like it. Although this *is* sharing the conflict, it is not really talking from the heart because it does not clearly reveal what the speaker is feeling. It may still be a perfectly fine thing to do.

The second half of talking from the heart is to clearly identify what the speaker wants. But what if the person has no idea what he or she wants? Well, that can be just fine, too. In sharing the conflict, the person can simply "tell it like it is" and trust that the next steps will become clear. Thus, a person can even say, "I feel a little uncomfortable right now. I'm not sure what I feel or even what I want us to be doing differently. I just wanted to put it out there and see what you all think." Another possibility might be "I am feeling a little uncertain right now. Anyone else feel that way?" Just sharing where a person is in this immediate moment and letting that be like the next domino laid on the table can be all that sharing the conflict entails. "Nature abhors a vacuum" is a well-known saying, and invariably something will happen to break the silence and get the group moving again. It is often a wonderful demonstration of synergism.

While there may be a great many situations in which a person might not know what to say, the simple formula that can apply to all of them is this: *when you don't know what to say, say so!* As people just share who they are in the spirit of friendship, the next step forward will invariably become clear.

Diplomacy Summarized

This chapter began with highlighting four important aspects of diplomacy, emphasizing that three are really just special applications of the first. Having spent some time now exploring each of the four, the key points and recommendations can be summarized as follows:

1. **Communicating so as to be well-received by the listener:** Lead with good intention (the desire to show caring and respect), and make it okay for others to feel whatever they feel. Ask questions that encourage clarification and expression; avoid generalizing the individual's experience; be careful not to put anyone on the spot; use a gentle approach, and always pair truth with kindness.

2. **Responding as opposed to keeping silent:** Silent spaces tend to be filled with negative assumptions, so make a point of responding to questions and messages; put reminders in your date book as to when a follow-up would be helpful; if there is nothing to report, just provide reassurance that the issue is being explored and hasn't been forgotten.

3. **Saying "no" in a way that preserves a positive relationship:** Include the four key elements that soften the blow by providing an explanation, offering an alternative, showing support of feelings, and inviting the other person's response.

4. **Knowing what to say when you don't know what to say:** When you don't know what to say, say so! Share the conflict by expressing what you feel, and trust that the next step forward will soon become clear.

In this last regard, one area where people often have difficulty knowing what to say is when others are expressing strong feelings—perhaps sadness, despair, fear, or anger. Let's look more closely at this application of diplomacy, beginning with one feeling that is almost always involved for parents when their children have special educational needs. What follows is an actual letter sent by such a parent.

THE GRIEF PROCESS

Grief is such an important aspect of having a child with a disability. It never goes away and it's always with me. I am still learning to not let it overwhelm me or to cloud my judgments, but there are times, even now, when I really have to shove it to the back of my heart.

I can tell you firsthand that grief is an integral part of how and why we parents make the educational decisions for our children. It may well be other emotions that drive the decisions we make, but when it all comes to a head, it's grief.

I don't think doctors or school staff even have a clue as to why parents' eyes glaze over when they first tell us that a child has a disability. I know when the results of my child's evaluation were read to me, I got stuck on the part when they said "mildly mentally retarded." I didn't hear a word they said after that. I looked at them and I'm sure I nodded and made the appropriate gestures, but I can't tell you a thing they said after that. For me, the grief cycle began at that moment and it hasn't stopped.

I have heard teachers complain after an IEP meeting and say, "I don't think that parent even listened to what I was saying." I just shake my head and then respond, "No, they probably didn't, but do you know why?"

Indeed, parents often perceive school officials and other professionals as not really understanding what they go through as parents of children with special needs. In the Introduction, this frequent concern was phrased this way:

Common emotional responses by parents, for whom an IEP meeting may be the first time they hear that their child has special needs (or hear specifics about the special needs), include shock, grief, fear, anger, mistrust, and guilt. Parents are typically not aware that these are to be expected, that their emotions will naturally be intense at times, and that there will be ongoing cycles of emotional response. **Parents too often feel alone with their feelings,** and school staff may be insufficiently aware of or supportive of the parents' emotions. Unless meaningfully addressed, these emotions can easily interfere with productive involvement in the IEP team. **Staff attending IEP team meetings**

would benefit from training in the emotional experience of parents and the grief process.

Collectively speaking, parents want help with their feelings—feelings they themselves may not understand and feelings that are certain to influence their participation as members of the IEP team. How, then, can team members show recognition and support of feelings in ways that help to overcome this common perception (or misperception) while at the same time serving the common goals of the team? Let's look at this question now.

As discussed in earlier chapters, feelings are motivators of behavior that will *always* be expressed somehow. Thus, whether parents even attend IEP meetings will depend on their feelings (intimidated versus included, belittled versus valued, empowered versus helpless, and so on). When they do attend, their feelings will determine how they participate (passively or actively, cooperatively or competitively). The degree to which they support the decisions of the team will also depend on their feelings (whether they trust the group or not, whether they feel comfortable with the decisions made). As mentioned in Chapter 1, the vision of the IEP team is one of sharing—sharing information, sharing in decision making, and sharing in the implementation of the decisions made. Clearly, the way the parents (and all team members) feel about what takes place will have everything to do with all three aspects of this collaborative vision.

The Unique Position of Parents as Team Members

In terms of the people aspect of principled negotiation, parents stand in a unique position within the team. The team is meeting, after all, for the benefit of *their* child. While all team members have certain goals and interests in common, they also have differences. For parents, theirs is a comprehensive responsibility, while the school's responsibilities are more narrowly defined (education), and parents have a lifelong and family relationship, as opposed to a more temporary and professional one. To the parents, the child is one of very few children (or perhaps just one alone), while to the school, he or she is invariably one of many. To understand the feelings of the parents broadens an awareness of the environment in which teams must work together. Such understanding raises the team's capacity to listen and support, which in turn adds to the strength and spirit of the team. Conversely, if teams do not understand how their members feel and do not recognize the importance of this issue, the probability of tensions, discord, and conflict becomes ever so much greater.

It may be worth briefly exploring the nature of grief and high-lighting some of the practical steps that IEP team members can take to provide support and assistance. Outlining those steps may also be helpful when, as described in the above letter, a parent is so emo-tionally overloaded that he or she can no longer actively participate in the meeting. Enhancing their understanding of a parent's experi-ence can strengthen the other team members' ability to know how to diplomatically respond—to know what to say when they might otherwise feel stuck. It must be emphasized, however, that the team is not expected to exceed its expertise or its role, which is to provide for the educational needs of the particular child. It is important not to lose sight of this overriding purpose.

Timelines and Power Points Reviewed

With the story of the frogs in Chapter 4, universal timelines were explored, emphasizing that emotions reflect mental responses and thus have only an *indirect* relationship to events. It can never, there-fore, be denied that feelings reflect thinking, and it would be an error to attribute anyone's feelings directly and solely to the cir-cumstances to which the feelings relate.

Thus, two parents hearing for the first time that their fifth-grade child is reading at a second-grade level may have very differ-ent feelings, depending on what they think (believe, expect, inter-pret, assume) about what they have heard. Timelines can be used to compare and contrast what happens as a result of their thinking, whether conscious or not, and whether in words or in imagery:

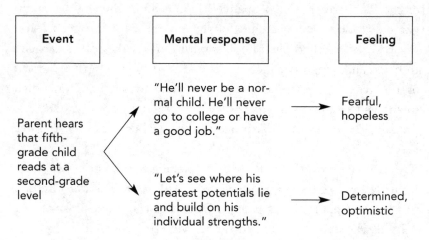

This universal relationship of emotion and thought is not always popular because most people have long been taught that the way they feel is shaped by events. This is undoubtedly a cardinal myth of the Western world because it saps people of so much of their power to achieve success and happiness in life. Furthermore, people can become accustomed to, and perhaps even comfortable with, the role of helplessness and believing that they have no power or control. If they allow this to happen, they may then vigorously resist efforts to help them take the steps necessary to move forward through their grief. A simple story may illustrate.

THE STORY OF THE TWIN SONS

Two sons were being interviewed about their lives. One was a terrible alcoholic, while the other was a teetotaller who never touched a drop of liquor.

The first son was asked, "Tell me, sir, your father and mother were both such heavy drinkers. How is it that you, too, have such a serious drinking problem?" And the first son replied, "With a family like I had, how could I be any different?"

The interviewer then asked the second son. "And you, sir, your mother was a heavy drinker, your father was a heavy drinker. Even your brother is a heavy drinker. How is it that you are a teetotaller and never touch a drop?" And the second son replied, "With a family like I had, how could I be any different?"

The obvious moral of the story is that it is not so much what happens to people in life that makes them who they are but what they choose to do with it—how they choose to think and act. These, once again, are the two primary power points.

Is this to suggest that parents shouldn't feel that way? Absolutely not! People should respect their feelings whatever they are, and work *with* them to restore positive feelings and positive thoughts, so that any unpleasant feelings are short-lived and help rather than hinder them in life.

Nature has endowed human beings with feelings for a reason, and every emotion is *good.* Negative emotions either call attention to faulty thinking that must be reviewed and revised, or they animate and impel toward constructive action in accordance with (hopefully) accurate perceptions. And each and every emotion serves a unique purpose in the toolbox of life. Grief serves the invaluable purpose of helping people to heal from what has been broken and so to prepare for the new—for whatever is coming next. Grief is to be expected whenever someone experiences loss, whether real or only perceived. At the same time, people must learn how to move through their grief, as opposed to getting stuck in it. The key lies in understanding how our systems work and in knowing the steps that can be taken to restore harmony when harmony is lost. Much of this becomes clear when we recognize who we really *are* and the five-point timelines we are living at every moment. In other words, people become most empowered when they understand that they *have* thoughts but are not their thoughts, experience emotions but are not their emotions, and have physical bodies but are not those bodies. As human beings, we are the inner selves, or *operators,* of mind, emotions, and bodies; how we choose to "operate" makes all the difference in life, which is the fundamental implication of the universal timeline.

Grieving as a Process

The special education environment provides many junctures where grief can be expected as a normal part of many parents' experience. It is likely to reemerge whenever there is an actual or perceived loss, which can happen at every major milestone on a child's educational journey. It can emerge whenever expectations are not met or whenever hopes are unfulfilled by new testing and new reports. It can surface again whenever a child is unable to do, experience, or accomplish what most age-appropriate peers can do. Because each individual is unique, what is easy for one parent to accept and resolve may be monumental for another.

One of the key challenges at every IEP meeting will be effectively managing the intensity of emotion that might otherwise interfere with goal achievement. The important question then becomes, "How can teams best help a member who is experiencing grief (or any other strong emotion), especially if those feelings are interfering with the productive work of the team?"

THE PERISTALTIC MOTION OF EMOTIONS

In Chapter 4, when behavioral alternatives for the expression of feelings were discussed, the analogy is presented of "draining the tub." To take this process a step further, it may be helpful to say a few words about *how* emotions "drain" and why unpleasant feelings must somehow find expression and resolution. An invaluable source of insight can be found in observing the peristalsis that occurs on a physical level and by noting that a parallel process occurs on an emotional.

Peristaltic motion is a well-known action in the physical body. It refers to the unceasing motion of the intestines as they absorb nutrients and push unusable material to be eliminated as waste. If we do not allow this process to occur, we "toxify." That is, the body begins to absorb waste matter, which then has an extremely injurious effect on the physical body.

How are such terms relevant to grief and the IEP environment? Well, in a parallel fashion, the emotional nature follows a very similar process whenever someone is feeling unpleasant emotions. These feelings stress the physical body and press for resolution, and those who do not resolve their grief will carry it with them until whatever time they do resolve it. This hanging on to unresolved negative feelings will always be at the expense of one's full capacity to experience the positive feelings that are otherwise hidden under layers of pain or negativity. The point, therefore, is that teams *must* support and respect the expression of unpleasant feelings—whether grief, anger, or whatever feelings they may be—for everyone's benefit. When intense emotions threaten the productivity of the team, the members must encourage their resolution by encouraging their expression.

SHOWING SUPPORT OF FEELINGS

Whenever people feel bad, they *will* express it somehow. By comparing different behavior trains, it becomes readily apparent that effective communication is usually the best of all options. For this reason, teams can be most helpful to a member who is feeling badly when they encourage open communication and offer support and understanding. Perhaps not surprising, the best way to do this is to begin with good listening skills.

All can hear but only the sensitive can understand. —Kahlil Gibran

In listening, it is important to do more than simply hear. A good listener will actively, openly, and genuinely *listen*. As discussed in Chapter 3, true listening shows support and caring, as well as valuing of the other person and his or her feelings. The listener may not always agree with the other person's thoughts but can always recognize the importance of showing respect and giving a moment of undivided attention. Before team members rush into defense, attack, explanation, or even trying to fix the problem, they can always encourage the person having strong feelings to express them and their associated thoughts. Each member of the team can also have an opportunity to share. It is a matter of timing—responding only after holding a focus, and then requesting permission before shifting from one person's perspectives to another's. Willingness (that great big W) is a major part of the process. Just being *willing* to show caring and respect will often go a long way toward achieving this important goal. Energy follows thought, and action follows intention.

As part of listening and striving for understanding, teams help each other enormously just by encouraging those who feel bad (and even those who feel good) to talk about their feelings. In so doing, bad feelings are usually ventilated as the speaker gets it off his or her chest. Once people acknowledge their feelings, the energy of those emotions tends to dissipate, as if they have served their fundamental purpose—to call attention to the thoughts they reflect, and/or to motivate the person into constructive action.

How exactly can teams do this? So often people step on each other's toes when they really don't intend to. How can teams show the support, caring, interest, and understanding that they would like to express? What words can be used to facilitate the process of acknowledging and sharing in a manner that both resolves bad feelings and effectively restores harmony and collaboration? In other words, how can teams diplomatically acknowledge feelings in a way that moves the group forward as opposed to keeping it stuck?

On the following page is a list of statements and questions that show support of feelings. In reviewing them, it is critically important to remember that *sincerity is essential.* If a person has the right words but the wrong spirit, it is likely that any good intention will not be heard. This can backfire terribly and go a long way to undermining the very trust and collaboration the speaker may be hoping to promote or restore. Unless a person really means what he or she is saying, the other person may feel manipulated and see the speaker as condescending. Once again, however, it all begins with willingness and the sincere desire to express understanding and support. Whenever people lead with that sincere desire, their good intention will usually be heard, above and beyond whatever words they may choose.

Words that Show Support of Feelings

"The more fully we can accept someone just to be where they are, the more easily they can take their next steps forward."

1. Say some more about that.
2. What was that like for you?
3. Help me understand your side of this.
4. How are you doing with that?
5. How did you feel when that happened?
6. I might feel that way, too, if I were in your shoes.
7. Is there anything else you want to say about that?
8. How would you have preferred that I handle it?
9. I really want to see it from your point of view.
10. I really want you to know that I care.
11. This seems to be really hard for you, right?
12. Guess you're wondering if we really care or want to help?
13. Sounds like you're kind of upset with me. Is that true?
14. Guess you're wondering if it would do any good, right?
15. Guess you're not sure if we're on your side, huh?

(continued)

16.   I'd really like to be helpful. What would be most helpful to you?

17.   I'm not sure what to say, but I want you to know that I care.

18.   I want you to think of me as available if you ever want to just talk.

19.   I really feel for you.

20.   I'm glad you're sharing your thoughts/feelings with me/us.

"It's not just the words but the music." *Sincerity is essential.*

Words to Avoid

There are also a number of statements and questions people often say that may reflect good intention and yet generally *do not* show support of feelings. It may be worth looking at some of these and considering why they may backfire, or at least why they may not be the best choices compared with those on the previous list. What follows now are some of the phrases best avoided. After each, there will be an explanation of why they are best avoided.

Avoid: I know how you feel.

Very often, this well-intentioned phrase will lead to an immediate response of "No, you don't!" This is especially likely when the person saying it is not standing, and perhaps never has stood, in the other person's shoes. It *might* be well received by, say, a parent of a child diagnosed with autism if it is said with sincere caring by *another parent* of a similarly diagnosed child. But if it is said by a school staff member who has no such child of his or her own, it is not likely to go over well. Sometimes the true motivation behind "I know how you feel" is really more one of "Can we please move on to other things?" If so, that *uncaring* intention is more likely to be heard than the words chosen to express it. Instead of "I know how you feel," the speaker is much safer in communicating the desire to be supportive by saying, "Tell us how you feel" or "How do you feel about that?"

or by providing similar opportunities for further expression. In other words, the idea is to open the door to further sharing, as opposed to doing or saying anything that might be seen as an effort to close it.

AVOID: I DON'T UNDERSTAND WHY YOU FEEL THAT WAY.

Even if no criticism is intended, how easy it might be to read into this statement, "I don't understand it because you shouldn't feel that way." The perception of judgments, whether really there or not, usually leads people to keep their feelings to themselves and to pull back from further participation—instead, they may withdraw behind a wall of bad feelings. Perhaps there is a better way to express the same good intention (to better understand the person's feelings). Because asking is affirming, another way of pursuing the same end might be, "Can you tell us more about that? What was it about that situation or statement that seemed inappropriate? How would you rather we had handled it?" If a person is honestly having trouble understanding, they can say so, perhaps by simply expressing the good intention: "I really want to understand your thoughts and feelings about that. I am having a little trouble. Can you help me?"

AVOID: BUT

Imagine if I said, "I see what you mean, but . . ." or "You have a point there, but . . ." Whenever someone qualifies a positive statement with a "but," it is almost like drawing a line through it and discounting whatever was said before. Most of the time, the "but" isn't really necessary, and the same statement can be made without any conjunction—as two independent thoughts—or by using "and" instead. As examples, compare and contrast the following:

I think testing might be a good idea, but I'm just not sure it will help.

I think testing might be a good idea. I'm just not sure it will help.

I think testing might be a good idea, and I'm just not sure it will help.

Avoid: What did that mean to you?

What something meant to the other person is often a very good question to ask, and yet note that it points toward what they perceived, interpreted, believed, or assumed—all of which are *mental* responses. While it may be a very good question in its right time, it should not be a first choice if the purpose is to show support of *feelings.* Furthermore, it may appear to contain another hidden judgment and to imply that the person shouldn't be seeing it that way. Instead, the same good intention can usually be accomplished more effectively by saying such things as, "Help me understand what that was like for you. Can you say some more about that? Can you help me see this from your point of view?"

Avoid: Why do you feel that way?

Once again there is a risk of appearing to be judgmental (even if the speaker is not) because "Why do you feel that way?" can easily be construed as "You shouldn't be feeling that way." As mentioned before, such perceived judgments are only likely to promote distance and additional bad feelings (such as shame, insecurity, or mistrust). Another risk is that "why" usually points away from feelings and into thoughts: *why* is a mentally-oriented question, as opposed to *how* and *what,* which tend to hold an encouraging focus on feelings.

IMPORTANT CAUTION

As a final note, it is important to emphasize that not all people are equally eager to explore or share their feelings! Many people are very reserved and even uncomfortable about getting close to their emotional sides, and so a large measure of both diplomacy and sensitivity is required in this area. For this reason, such questions or statements as "How did you feel emotionally?" or "Were you feeling sad?" may seem very threatening to some people, especially in a group setting where they may already be feeling less than comfortable. A helpful option is therefore to provide "cushions" that allow people to share their feelings only to the extent that they feel comfortable to do so. Certain statements or questions from the previous list of options may thus be more safe than others, in that they are less likely to put anyone in what might be perceived as an awkward or vulnerable position. As an example, I am less likely to arouse defenses if I ask you, "Can you tell me more about your side of this?" than if I say, "Sounds like you really felt threatened by her remark." Similarly, I may be safer asking you, "What was it like for you when that happened?" as opposed to "Sounds like you really felt hurt when she said that." The way things are said is so very important, not just in showing support of feelings, but in all our communications with others.

This chapter began with the story of a sultan and his wise men. Although there is no guarantee how any particular sultan will respond, we can now fairly safely predict what will be more or less *likely* to get teams into trouble—and perhaps even ensure them some handsome rewards.

Chapter 6

The Search
for Serenity

S ometimes, despite the team's best efforts at being efficient and professional, respectful and diplomatic, conflicts will arise. This by itself is not a problem. The more important issue is what the members will *do* with their conflicts and whether they use them to strengthen or weaken the team. Fortunately, conflict resolution is usually not difficult, and some of the keys to success build upon what has already been discussed while some may appear brand new.

The basic elements of conflict resolution can be conveniently summarized in terms of a triad—a three-sided thing—based on the very familiar saying:

> Grant me the serenity to accept the things I cannot change,
> the courage to change the things I can,
> and the wisdom to know the difference.

Some may wonder what serenity has to do with the IEP environment, and the question can be answered in several ways. First, there is, of course, no technique or approach that will guarantee success and happiness in every situation. There will be times when, despite the best of efforts and intentions, the desired results simply cannot be achieved, and when that happens, there may be no choice but to live with it—to adopt "the serenity to accept the things we cannot change." A word of caution, though: sometimes people draw this conclusion prematurely, before they have really done all that they *can do* to resolve or improve the situation at hand. That having been said, being able to adopt serenity when faced with situations that really cannot be changed is certainly a valuable skill to have.

Another relevance of serenity in the IEP environment has to do with the qualities being brought to the table. That is, whether the team members bring a calming and peaceful presence to the meeting or one of pressure, intensity, and tension. Do the team members carry themselves in ways that promote the kind of relaxed and comfortable atmosphere that is more pleasant for all involved while enhancing the efficiency and harmony of the team? The fact is that the emotional energy level of the members can do a great deal to set the tone for the meeting, and there is a contagious effect. Members can lead the way through their own example and either help to "still the waters" or to agitate them just by the qualities they bring to the mix within the room.

Another feature of serenity has to do with the ability to remain calm and relaxed even when others are not. In this way, teams are most likely to keep their heads and make wise decisions. In addition, staying relaxed helps any individual to *respond* as opposed to react. That is, people are more likely, when they remain relaxed, to respond to the others at the meeting, as opposed to "getting buttons pushed" and moving into defensive reactions that may escalate tensions and not really be helpful.

A final thought regarding the relevance of serenity is that it makes for a better day. The opposite of maintaining serenity is maintaining tension, and this takes energy, stresses the body, and has a tiring effect, all of which are just not fun. I have heard from a number of people that, for them, the most valuable part of the "Collaboration in the IEP Environment" workshop was simply becoming aware of how much tension they tend to carry and learning some specific techniques to help them stay more calm and relaxed.

The relevance of serenity to the IEP environment can be summarized as follows:

1. Promoting an atmosphere conducive to harmony and enjoyment

2. Avoiding the contagious effect of tension, pressure, and intensity

3. Facilitating clear thinking and wise decision making

4. Maintaining the ability to respond as opposed to react

5. Minimizing stress to the physical body

6. Finding peace when, despite the team's best efforts, success is not reached

If this sounds like a good list of reasons, the question then becomes how a team can best achieve serenity—how *can* they adopt serenity in the often fast-paced, challenging, and sometimes emotionally charged IEP environment?

THE IMPORTANCE OF SELF-AWARENESS

With awareness comes the ability to make flexible choices.

This very meaningful saying is a central feature of Gestalt psychology, a school of thought that places a heavy emphasis on being aware of one's feelings and one's physical body. The basic idea is that when people know what they are feeling, what they are doing, how it is working, and what their options are, they become empowered to decide whether they want to continue the same way or, instead, to try something different. That is, with self-awareness, a person can make what the Gestaltists call the "growth choice" as opposed to the more familiar and often more comfortable "fear choice." Conversely, when people are unaware, they are very limited in their options. Without self-awareness, they remain stuck and at the mercy of their habits.

So where does one get serenity? Obviously, serenity is not something one can simply go out and buy or just find on any beach or mountainside. People can, theoretically, be just as nervous and worried on a beach in the Bahamas as they can in their offices, classrooms, or homes. Obviously, serenity is an *internal* experience, and if people want serenity, they will have to learn how to find it within their very own selves. Perhaps the analogy of the eye of a tornado will help to clarify how true this really is.

THE EYE OF THE TORNADO

Scientists have long understood that within every tornado or hurricane is a center of perfect stillness, referred to as the *eye* of the tornado. Despite the whirling turbulence and destruction outside, this center is always calm. Similarly, within each and every human being is a center of peace that can be accessed at any time we choose to, if we only know how. Once we do know how, we can maintain our serenity despite whatever may be going on around us. Serenity is thus not something to be created. Like the eye of the tornado, it is always there and need only be *found.* Fortunately, this can be accomplished very easily with just a little practice, and as mentioned above, the first steps begin with awareness.

This chapter explores several techniques aimed at both raising awareness and finding that eye of the tornado in the stillness within. A variety of approaches will be presented, including breathing awareness, three forms of relaxation exercises, and positive thinking.

BREATHING AWARENESS

What could be more simple and seem less necessary than to become aware of one's breathing? Yet there is a great deal to be gained in this regard. An exercise I often do with workshop participants is to ask them to count the number of breaths they take in 30 seconds, with each breath in and each one out counting as one breath. What I invariably find is a bell-shaped curve, where most people are in the

5–7 range, a few lower, and several higher. The ones who report the lowest breathing rates are usually those who have taken training in meditation, yoga, or similar techniques designed to enhance relaxation skills. But what about those scoring 8, 10, 12, or even more?

Well, two things are very much noteworthy with these rapid breathers. The first is that not only are they breathing more quickly but their breathing is also more shallow. In other words, they are using only a small part of their full lung capacity (which is true for most of us most of the time, though to differing degrees). The second noteworthy observation is that this counting exercise takes place in what most people would consider a very nonthreatening and comfortable atmosphere—sitting as a participant in a workshop, quietly observing one's breathing. What would you think is predictable if this same counting exercise were performed while driving on slippery roads or in heavy traffic while late for a meeting? What would it be while watching an exciting basketball game? And what would it be while sitting in an emotionally charged and conflict-laden IEP meeting? The easily demonstrated point is that a person's breathing changes with the circumstances (more precisely, with changing responses to differing circumstances), and it will almost always become more shallow and more rapid in any setting of probable stress. Does it matter? Absolutely!

If I ask any group of people to simply take three deep breaths—all the way down to their pockets—it is a golden guarantee that a strange kind of quiet will come over the group. Like "hearing a pin drop," the room full of 5, 50, or 500 people will suddenly become so very serene that it is almost tangible. It is truly amazing and yet so very simple. The point is that a major avenue for adopting the serenity that is always *potentially* accessible is simply to do what we have been doing every day of our lives: breathe! Psychologists have coined the phrase *maintaining the relaxation response,* and its enormous significance lies in the fact that as long as a person maintains relaxation on a physical level, fear, anxiety, and other emotional reactivity simply cannot take hold.

The analogy of a sailboat can be helpful in illustrating this very important and yet simple process. When a sailboat glides along on the water, only a part of it can be seen—much like the tip of the proverbial iceberg. What is *not* seen is that which keeps it stable: the keel.

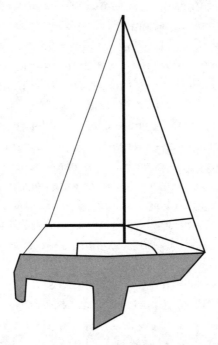

The keel is like a blade, usually filled with weight (ballast), and it extends into the water for the purpose of keeping the boat stable despite any turbulence of the wind or waves. The size of the keel is very apparent when a boat is out of the water, in dry dock for paint or repairs or on a trailer being transported down the highway. Just as the keel is the stabilizer of the boat, without which the boat might easily tip over, breathing serves a similar purpose for all human beings: Deep and rhythmic breathing helps to keep us stable despite whatever turbulence may be threatening to tip *us* over.

Some Native Americans have an interesting term for psychologists. They call them "wind-water dancers." In their view, the universe is composed of four primary elements (earth, water, wind, and fire), which interestingly correspond to the holistic model of physical, emotional, mental, and spiritual. Psychologists work in the realms of mind and emotion, hence "wind-water dancers." Isn't it curious how breathing serves to stabilize people in mind and emotion just as keels stabilize sailboats in wind and water!

The "moral of the story" is to stay aware of one's breathing. As a first step toward stress management at IEP meetings, any team member can simply take a deep breath or two. Nobody will see the person doing it, and it doesn't cost a penny, yet the benefits are enormous. When team members maintain the relaxation response, first through deep and rhythmic breathing, they are very likely to notice how much more clearly they can think, how much more serenity they maintain and promote, how much more productively they work with others, and how much more enjoyable and stress-free they find their meetings to be. These are big dividends from such a very small investment!

RELAXATION EXERCISES

The second key element of the relaxation response (and of adopting serenity) is muscular relaxation. This means letting the muscles remain loose and heavy and not allowing oneself to hold unnecessary tension. Recall for a moment the five-point universal timeline of event, mental response, feeling, behavior, and consequence. It is time now to look more closely at the transition between feeling and behavior.

All emotions are animators of behavior—they motivate us (always) into some form of action. As part of this universal process, *every emotion is reflected in the physical body.* Thus, when people feel happy, they may smile or laugh and perhaps even sing. Any of these are very *obvious* reflections of emotions on a physical level. Careful observation will reveal that such positive emotions also have less obvious reflections: perhaps a person feels taller, as if being lifted by invisible strings, or his breathing becomes deeper, as if he were lazing in a hammock on a warm, spring day, or his shoulders feel light and airy, as if there were a gentle breeze blowing across them. Such self-awareness may not be readily apparent to anyone for whom this is a brand new subject, but it can be golden guaranteed with just a little time and attention. Indeed, it is a universal truth that emotions *always* have physical counterparts. They are reflected in such obvious expressions as breathing rate and depth, muscular tension, tones of voice, body postures and gestures, and facial expressions. They are also reflected in a host of less obvious physical responses, such as blood pressure, heart rate, and endocrine secretions. This is equally true for negative (unpleasant) emotions as positive (pleasant) emotions.

Breathing has been compared to the keel of a sailboat. A very similar process with equally powerful benefits involves maintaining relaxation on a physical level—simply letting all the muscles go loose and heavy—not just in quiet moments of inward reflection but in moments of turbulence. In other words, people benefit greatly by learning to maintain physical relaxation in potentially stressful situations when emotions run high, tempers flare, voices are raised, and so on. As mentioned before, team members will contribute greatly to maintaining serenity for themselves *and* promoting serenity for others when they stay relaxed, and starting on a physical level is a major first step.

So how exactly does one do it? Well, there are a broad variety of exercises and techniques that can be helpful, and practicing any of them for as little as 5 or 10 minutes per day can have dramatic results. Three of the most common categories of relaxation exercises will be presented below. Feel free to choose the exercise that works best for you or to develop a blend of your own.

Begin each of the following by finding a comfortable place where you will not be disturbed for the 5 to perhaps 20 minutes during which you want to focus on the exercise. Sitting in a comfortable chair with eyes closed is recommended. If you have a tendency to fall asleep, try sitting on the edge of a chair with your back not supported or on a cushion on the floor. A firm statement to yourself, also known as an *affirmation,* can also be very helpful, such as "This exercise is important to me. I *will* stay aware! I *will* stay awake!"

Exercise 1: Progressive Muscle Relaxation

This exercise involves alternately tensing and then relaxing each and every muscle group from head to toe, each time becoming clearly aware of what it feels like to hold tension in that area and then what it feels like to experience relaxation in that area. The steps can be typed out as follows, but it may work much more effectively, at least the first few times, to have someone read these to you *slowly* while you just follow along with eyes closed. Similar exercises are also available on cassette, CD, and video, which can be purchased at a bookstore or borrowed from a library. (You could even make a relaxation tape of your own.)

1. Make a fist in both hands and feel the tension. Let yourself be aware of what it feels like to hold tension in your hands, wrists, and fingers. Then relax and note the difference.

2. Tense your biceps by "making a muscle" with your upper arms. Hold the tension for a moment. Then relax, and note the difference.

3. Straighten your arms out behind you—tight and tense. Feel the tension in the back of your arms. Hold it for a moment. And now relax and note the difference.

4. Scrunch up your face by pressing your jaws, lips, and eyes together. Feel the tension throughout your facial muscles. Hold it, and be keenly aware of what tension feels like in the muscles of your face. Again, relax, and allow yourself to clearly perceive the difference between tension and relaxation.

5. Continue this same procedure, slowly and deliberately progressing through each of the major muscle groups, including neck, shoulders, chest, stomach, hips, buttocks, thighs, calves, feet,

and toes. With each area, tighten and tense for a moment and feel that tension clearly, then relax and notice the difference.

Exercise 2: Relaxation through Observation and Self-Suggestion

In contrast to the previous technique, relaxation through observation and self-suggestion involves no actual tensing of muscles. Here, a person simply observes each area of the body, becoming aware of any tension he or she may be holding there, and then simply allowing that area to become more relaxed and comfortable just by letting it go. In a sense, this exercise involves learning how to "play dead" or "make like a wet dishcloth" that simply takes the shape of whatever is holding it up. This relaxation through observation and self-suggestion is done in stages, going from one part of the body to the next, slowly and methodically, from head to toe.

1. Carefully observe the muscles of your forehead and scalp. Be aware of any tension you may be holding there. If you discover any tension, allow it to dissolve and let this area move more and more fully into a state of perfect peace.

2. Now focus on the muscles of your eyebrows and eyes. Be aware of any subtle tensions you may be holding in these areas. If you discover any tension whatsoever, let that tension go. Let these areas be fully relaxed. Simply allow yourself—give yourself permission—to move more fully into a state of total relaxation, comfort, and peace.

3. Proceed through each and every area of your body, slowly and carefully observing, and then purposely, yet effortlessly, letting go, allowing each area to become more and more fully at peace. Take your time and proceed at your own pace, without any hurry whatsoever. Simply observe, be aware, and then release, let go, and allow yourself to move ever more fully into a state of perfect rest.

Exercise 3: Relaxation through Affirmation and Creative Visualization

A third relaxation exercise involves taking a mental journey through a series of very restful images, and it lends itself very well to your own individual design. It begins with the selection of a setting that is particularly relaxing for you personally. For some people, the most relaxing scenario imaginable might be lying on a beach in the Bahamas, while someone else might prefer sitting on a mountaintop looking off into the distance. Another person might prefer to think of lounging in a hot bubble bath, perhaps with a favorite book. The imagery doesn't even have to be real—you could imagine sitting in a fluffy cloud and being surrounded by a golden light of peace energy. It doesn't matter what the imagery is, as long as it helps you to relax and to feel, right here and now, as much serenity as you can find. An important point is that the more you practice this, the more you will be able to tap into it at any time, even when not in your own quiet and private room or office—any time you turn toward the eye of the tornado where there is always calm within the storm.

1. Let all of your muscles go loose and comfortable, and to the best of your ability, relax. In a sense, play dead and let your whole body become like a wet dishcloth that simply takes the shape of whatever is holding it up. Affirm to yourself silently and with real conviction, "I give myself permission to use this time to fully relax and be at peace."

2. Mentally imagine that you are surrounded by a bubble of soft, white light, as if you were sitting inside a fluffy, white cloud of peace energy.

3. Imagine that with each breath in, you are breathing in the quality of peace and that with each breath out, you are exhaling the quality of peace. See this light of peace flowing throughout your whole being, bringing a deep sense of comfort to every part of your body, a serenity and tranquility to your emotions, a stillness and calmness to your mind.

4. Affirm to yourself slowly, silently, and with as much conviction as you can, "I am at peace. I am relaxed. With every breath, I allow myself to move more and more fully into a state of total rest. I release all thoughts, all cares, all tensions, all tightness. All of my muscles are deeply relaxed, and I am immersed in the presence and power of peace. I am surrounded by the quality of peace, and nothing but peace can be where I am now."

5. Continue with similar statements and imagery for 5–20 minutes.

A Second Example of Creative Visualization

Imagine yourself sitting beside a soothing, gentle waterfall, listening to the sounds of nature: the birds in the nearby trees, the gentle sound of the breeze. Imagine yourself bathed in the warmth of the sunshine, far away from all turbulence, all cares, all concerns. Silently affirm that you are in your special place of serenity, soothed by beauty and peace. Continue with similar thoughts and imagery.

Relaxation exercises using affirmation and creative visualization are by now widely used and readily available. As mentioned before, many cassettes, CDs, and videos are available to assist in this endeavor and can be found at libraries, music stores, health food stores, and bookstores.

POSITIVE THINKING FOR RELAXATION

At several points in earlier chapters, the importance of positive thinking has been emphasized, as well as how powerfully thoughts shape feelings and behaviors. It only follows, therefore, that if any team member hopes to feel peaceful and relaxed, then positive thinking will be of critical importance. This subject has been covered so fully in earlier chapters that it need only be referenced now with a couple of specific recommendations.

Relax, breathe, and think positively.

This simple trio is the first line of defense in any challenging or conflict situation. Before any other steps are taken, before any techniques are chosen, before any response is made, these are the immediate action steps anyone can take that will by themselves make a great and positive difference. For many people, however, the initial tendency is just the opposite: to tighten the muscles and to either hold one's breath or let the breathing become more rapid and shallow. Many people also have a tendency to lead with negative thoughts, such as "Oh, no, not again!" or "I don't need this kind of grief!" or some other past-based, automatic, and *limiting* mental response. Instead, team members can begin to form the habit of letting their first response be one of "We can work it out," "I can handle this," or a similar *positive* thought that will set a positive direction and serve as an inner pep talk.

The supreme importance of projecting positive expectations relates to what has been called *the self-fulfilling prophecy,* which simply highlights that what one expects, one tends to get. Teachers know how important it is for a student to believe that he or she can do well in a particular subject and how destructive it can be for any student to expect failure. With such an understanding in mind, team members can put this fundamental principal to work *for them,* rather than against them, by intentionally projecting the expectation of success, harmony, understanding, and any of the positive features they would like to see characterize their IEP meetings. Expecting success promotes success, just as expecting conflict, tension, difficulty, and adversity tends to promote the same. Positive thinking is a habit (a *good* habit), and for some, it may be very challenging to expect wonderful IEP meetings. There is an old and valuable saying that "what were once cobwebs are now cables." Like riding a bicycle, what starts with only great care and attention can soon become easy and even second nature.

As a final note, it may be worth emphasizing once again *why* relaxation should be a focus of all IEP teams. The ability to maintain serenity is, in any conflict scenario, one of the three cornerstones of the conflict resolution triad. Maintaining serenity promotes clear thinking and strengthens the ability of team members to listen and respond supportively to one another, as opposed to reacting and defending against one another. A relaxed environment promotes a positive climate at IEP meetings, making the workday that much more pleasant and enjoyable for all involved. Small wonder that many participants in conflict resolution workshops have reported that learning to stay relaxed and to think positively are among the most valuable benefits they received.

Chapter 7

The Courage
to Make Changes

The title of this chapter comes, of course, from the second line of the triad of conflict resolution: "the courage to change the things I can." But courage without skill has little chance of success; the two go very much together. When courageous people know what they can do and how they can do it, they are much more likely to be able to do it successfully when the time to act arrives. An often quoted phrase from the military is "We fight the way we train." Perhaps in the IEP environment, teams can train to fight cooperatively, productively, with mutual respect, and with their common interests always in mind.

Some people see conflict as inherently bad and best avoided, and they see fighting as one of the worst things that any team could possibly do. Yet conflict sometimes goes with the territory in the IEP environment, and it need not be awful, frightening, or inherently unpleasant. Conflict can be expected from time to time whenever people have strong emotions, feel stressed or pressured, hold different expectations, or have a different understanding. The good news is that conflict can be the very avenue through which feelings are resolved, pressures are eased, expectations are realigned, and understanding becomes shared. When used productively, conflict can actually strengthen teams, and this chapter offers some specific techniques for making this very realistic goal entirely possible.

It may seem to some readers that the techniques for intervening in conflict are the real meat of this book. However, although it is certainly important to have a variety of skills for intervention, such skills must not be approached in isolation. It is important to understand that intervention strategies are, of necessity, curative rather than preventative. Mastering intervention techniques alone is like learning how to put out fires when it is so much better to prevent the fires from getting started in the first place. Many a conflict will be avoided or minimized through mastery of many topics *other than* intervention skills (such as meeting management, diplomacy, listening skills, and so on). With that said, this chapter addresses what specifically *can* be done when conflict threatens to emerge or has already developed.

THE THREE NO-NOS

Of course, it is essential to be careful when it comes to generalizations. At the same time, I have been struck by the frequency and consistency with which school personnel tend to reach for three identifiable intervention options, often at the expense of a wide variety of others. These three are

1.   Educating

2.   Rushing to "fix it"

3.   Using "the hands"

Educating is simply the process of giving helpful explanations. It is a perfectly acceptable and even important thing to do. The key, however, is in the timing and being sure that the others involved are willing and *ready to listen.* More is said about this in a moment.

"Fix it" is the process of problem solving, and most school professionals are very skilled in this regard. (It is often a prerequisite for the job!) Again, however, there is a need for attention to timing and to the *process,* as opposed to just the outcome. For collaboration to be safe-guarded, it is important to allow members a chance to share, discuss, explore, and participate before heading straight for the conclusions.

"The hands" refers to patting gestures that are often used and may inadvertently be seen as an effort to suppress and control, as if saying, "Hold on, settle down, and just listen." Once the hands are identified at workshops, the participants usually have some good laughs about them, especially during role-playing, when some school professionals will literally sit on their hands so no one can see them playing "paddy cake"—the habit can be just that hard to break. The option, of course, is more up-turned, open, and welcoming gestures, as if inviting participants to speak up and say more.

It is true for all people that, as they grow through their expe-riences and learn from their role models, they develop particular sets of skills. These skill sets are the ones they will (understandably) reach for first when they feel threatened or attacked and must take action to prevent or resolve conflict. The only problem is that very often these lists of options are short ones, and people quickly become frustrated and discouraged when the options they reach for do not meet the needs at hand. Team members do well, therefore, to con-tinually review, revise, and expand their lists of options so that they become increasingly skilled at responding to the many and some-times unexpected situations they will face in the course of their pro-fessional lives. The Japanese business philosophy of *kaizen*—mean-ing continual improvement—fits very well in this regard.

EXPANDING THE LIST OF SKILLS

From brainstorming with hundreds of IEP team members, a long list of possible response options has emerged. Many of these will look familiar, and readers may find themselves saying, "Oh, yes, I do that." Some workshop participants have commented on how affirm-ing it is for them to be able to define a particular response that they use—to be able to give it a name and so to bring into focus an option they already have in their toolboxes. Such labels can also be helpful in providing a framework in which to compare and contrast the many options available in a given situation. Presented on the following pages are no fewer than 25 prevention/intervention options. Team members can rapidly develop new skills by recognizing the many options from which to choose and by practicing those options until they become both familiar and comfortable with each. A summary for easy reference is presented at the end of this chapter.

Consider again the saying that it's not just the words but the music. It is critically important that the use of these techniques includes the right attitude of caring, respect, and a genuine desire to work together cooperatively toward common goals. On the one hand, techniques employed without the proper spirit and intention can quickly be perceived as patronizing and manipulative. Sometimes they will be perceived that way *even with* the proper intention. On the other hand, given the right attitude, whatever a person does will often have a safety net. That is, when a person's heart is truly in the right place, whatever is said will usually be well received. Because of the basic principle that action follows intention, team members should always be sure to lead with good intention and to let their words and behavior, whatever they may be, follow from that.

25 INTERVENTION OPTIONS

1. **Share the conflict:** Express your own feelings and trust that the next steps will become clear. Example: "I feel kind of attacked right now. I'm not sure how to proceed."

Mark Twain is quoted as saying, "If you tell the truth, you don't have to remember anything." Sharing the conflict is such a valuable skill because it requires nothing more than sharing what you feel right here and now! Remember, though, that feelings are always one word and that phrases such as "feel like," "feel that," "feel as if," and "feel as though" invariably point toward thoughts, not feelings. Sharing the conflict is just a matter of taking whatever you are feeling inside and sharing it with the group. What could be more simple? Yet watch how very helpful it can be. Several examples of this invaluable skill are presented in Chapter 5, where it is also said that "nature abhors a vacuum." When a team member allows tension just to be for a moment and puts it out there for the group to consider, it is amazing how predictably someone will fill the vacuum with something that helps the team move forward once again.

2. **Hold a focus:** Ask for more at least twice, then ask to respond. Example: "Is there anything else you'd like to say? [Allow a response.] Anything else I should understand about this? [Allow a response.] May I respond to what you've said?"

Holding a focus is, of course, one of the four keys to effective communication that are discussed in Chapter 4. It simply involves taking turns—one person and one topic at a time. The purpose is to provide an opportunity for the other person to clarify the issues of concern, to express thoughts and feelings, and to get it off the chest so as to dissipate the intensity of emotion. Sincerely holding a focus communicates caring, respect, and a desire to listen and be helpful. Such real listening is uncommon in Western culture. (Most people tend to be much better talkers than listeners.) For most people, therefore, the ability to hold a focus will be a skill they need to make a conscious effort to improve. Yet, for many reasons, it is both important and well worth the effort. The one holding a focus will also have a turn to speak and to share—hopefully after listening carefully and then asking permission to shift from the other person's thoughts, feelings, and concerns to his or her own.

At times, it may seem that tensions actually *rise* when people are encouraged to talk about their feelings. Usually, this is only because they haven't really pulled the plug on their tub full of feelings the first time around, and getting it off their chests only starts with the second or third encouragement of their self-expression. Very rarely will it require more than two or three rounds of encouragement before the intensity of emotion begins to subside as the tub begins to drain.

3. **Paraphrase and reflect:** Simply repeat back what you are hearing. Example: "Let me see if I understand what you're saying. You think Sally's classroom teacher is really unfair and the school is not really giving your daughter the quality of education we're required to give?"

Notice that to do this requires the listener to avoid becoming defensive and argumentative. Instead, the goal is to just allow the other person's thoughts, perceptions, and feelings to be simply and clearly heard for a moment. Doing so can provide several important benefits. The first is to offer an opportunity for the other party to clarify any misperceptions on the listener's part. (Perhaps the speaker will clarify: "No, that's not quite what I meant.") Second, the listeners show (if their hearts are in the right place) that they are listening without judgment and are sincerely trying to understand, which by themselves can have a very positive influence on communication and team spirit. Finally, when people are truly being unreasonable, they usually don't have to be told. They will often see it for themselves if someone can just "mirror" for them what it is they are saying. This is not, however, to discount the potential value of their feedback; the listeners, too, can benefit from really hearing whatever is being said. Very often, there is at least a germ of truth, and all team members should strive to be open to at least hearing and considering it, if they are truly committed to being team players and sharing and learning together.

A word of caution: Try not to change the speaker's words. If someone says, "I think you sometimes expect too much," it is not paraphrasing if the listener takes a defensive tone and replies, "Oh, so now you're saying I'm incompetent?" When it comes to paraphrasing, the challenge is to stay as close to the speaker's words as possible and to play the role of mirror, not adversary. In this example, the listener could respond with "Let me see if I'm following you. You think I sometimes expect too much."

4. **Educate:** Give explanations, perhaps about policies, laws, and so on. Example: "We cannot transfer children to other schools unless their needs really cannot be met where they currently are."

The option of educating was mentioned before as one of the three common no-nos of school personnel. While educating is definitely a valid option, a few points are worth considering. To respond to feelings with information is very often the first (but not best) line of defense. That is, many school personnel are quick to explain what district policy is or what the law states or what it is they are required to do. Those who are educators are, after all, professionals at the process of giving information, and it comes very easily to them. However, if they move into educating before the other party is really ready to listen, what they will get is likely to be walls, defenses, and a good but unproductive game of tug-of-war—not true listening and sharing and not collaboration leading to consensus. Education is fine. It is even important. Once again, timing is the key issue. As most educators would surely agree, there is little to be gained by educating if the student is not open and listening *first*.

5. **Confront the individual:** Objectively point out a person's disturbing behavior. Example: "Sally, I notice that you are raising your voice right now."

Confrontation, whether gentle or sharp, is indeed another option among the many in the toolbox. And it is one with which most people are very familiar. But is it the best choice? Many times it will not be because it has some definite downsides. First, it singles out one member of the group. Second, if it contains negative feedback, it is likely to be taken as belittling, embarrassing, and even hurtful. It is therefore unlikely to build team spirit and more likely to lead to defensiveness, counterattacks, or withdrawal. Like the hammer in the toolbox when a fly swatter would do, confrontation is best reserved for when it really is necessary. Usually there are much safer alternatives. Also, when it *does* seem necessary to confront a member of the team, it will be important to do so in the most respectful, supportive, and gentle way possible. Confrontation will usually only be a good choice after other, softer options have been tried without success. Assuming that confrontation does seem the best option in a given situation, consider the following alternatives:

Mrs. Jones, you are being needlessly rude and disrespectful.

Mrs. Jones, you are obviously upset with something we said.

Mrs. Jones, you are raising your voice.

Mrs. Jones, you seem a little upset with something. Would you help me understand your thoughts? [pairing gentle confrontation with asking for help]

6. **Confront the group:** Make comments about the group rather than the individual. Example: "Are we clearly on task right now?"

Instead of confronting the individual, notice that confronting the group can raise the same issues without pointing fingers at anyone in particular. This can often accomplish the same objectives without putting anyone on the spot. Once again, when confronting *does* seem the best choice, it can be done most effectively with a gentle and respectful touch. Note how phrasing the confrontation as a question ("Are we on task?") rather than a statement ("We are off task") can also have a softening effect.

7. **Reflect/invite to the group:** Share an observation and ask the group to assist. Example: "We seem to be kind of quiet right now. Any ideas how we might move through this?"

Very similar to option 6 (confront the group), this option differs in the focus being not so much on where the group is at the moment but instead on how it can move forward. The invitation is for the group to recommend the steps it would suggest taking. Asking is affirming, and this option is generally a very safe one.

8. **Take a break:** A short break can provide time for tempers to cool. Example: "I wonder if a 5-minute leg stretch might be a good idea right now."

Although taking a break is certainly an option to consider, there are reasons to be very selective in reaching for it, partly because time is so precious. The team members have cleared their schedules and managed to arrange for class or childcare coverage, transportation, and so on. For this reason alone, releasing the group should best be avoided unless absolutely necessary. One of the risks that goes with taking a break is that some team members may disappear and it may be difficult to get them all back together. What is also important is that time marches on, and the time spent on breaks is that much less time available to focus on the agenda of the meeting.

9. **Caucus:** Provide time for small-group or individual discussion. Example: "Mrs. Jones, would it be helpful to take a little time for just you and me to talk in private?"

The private discussion is always an option, and yet it bears all the same risks as taking a break—lost members, lost focus, and lost time. In addition, not all members are privy to whatever is being discussed in the private meeting, so there may be additional time required later to bring everyone up to date. Furthermore, it is human nature to fill the spaces with fantasies, so if John and Mary are talking out in the hallway, the other members are left to wonder and imagine what it is they are talking about. Unless team spirit and trust are strong, such private discussion can weaken rather than strengthen the meeting. Instead, it may be best to reserve private discussion for when really necessary, such as when strong emotions, hot tempers, or decision-making impasse otherwise threaten the achievement of the goals for the day.

10. **Probe for underlying interests:** Explore reasons so as to gain understanding. Example: "This issue seems to be very important to you, and you must have good reasons. Can you help us understand your thoughts about that?"

This option has a lot to recommend it, with no known negative side effects. It fits well with both principled negotiation and holding a focus. It communicates caring, interest, respect, and inclusion. It assumes good thinking and leads with a positive expectation ("You must have good reasons"), rather than with suspicion or criticism ("What good would that do?"). It also helps to bring thoughts, perceptions, and beliefs into focus, which is a very central role of partnership (the sharing of information and decision making). Two enthusiastic thumbs up for this one.

11. **Affirm:** Use praise as a means of support (perhaps along with another technique). Example: "I think you've raised some valid concerns there."

This option can be helpful in showing interest and respect; it is best not to negate it by following with a *but,* as in "You've raised some good points, but . . ." or "I agree with what you say, but . . . ." Compare and contrast these with "You've raised some good points there. I agree with much of what you've said, and I have a few questions. What do you see happening in terms of . . . ?" Using *and* or two separate sentences with no conjunction at all helps to minimize the perception of negating any positive thoughts. A second caveat, once again, is the importance of sincerity: If praise is only setting the stage for countering what has been said, there is a great risk of the music drowning out the words. The one giving praise may be perceived as manipulative and condescending, which can really undermine team spirit and trust. By all means, use praise and positive statements liberally, *and* let them be sincere expressions of a desire to build up the team and to highlight valid thoughts, perceptions, and suggestions, even when they may not yet be a perfect finished product.

12. **Point at self:** Let any perceived ignorance, impatience, and so on be directed at you to avoid putting anyone else in an uncomfortable position. Example: "I'm not sure I am following you, Mrs. Jones. Could you rephrase that for me, please?"

This option allows a safety net, in contrast to pointing fingers at others. A classic example, albeit exaggerated, is the team member who only means to help the parent (Mrs. Smith) by saying to the diagnostician, "Mr. Frank, I really don't think Mrs. Smith could possibly understand all that school jargon. For her benefit, would you please repeat that in everyday language that she can understand?" While Mrs. Smith *might* feel eternally grateful for this extra attention and special consideration, it is also very possible that she will feel singled out as the only one on the team who cannot follow the terminology and that she will feel more embarrassed than supported. Why run the risk? By pointing at self, it is very unlikely that anyone will feel set apart or belittled.

Some may question whether this is really honest, especially if the one asking the question really is following what the speaker said. Diplomacy must certainly begin with honesty, and yet just as in the story of the sultan and his wise men (Chapter 5), there are always many honest ways to express whatever it is that needs to be said. Other options within this same example might include "Excuse me, Mr. Frank, I just want to be sure I understand those acronyms the same way you do. Can you rephrase that for me in everyday terms?" or "It would really help me to hear those acronyms in everyday terms. Could I trouble you to repeat that last part again in different words?" There are always options. The point is to avoid singling out any one member of the team or saying anything that might be construed as critical. By pointing at oneself, such perceptions are far less likely to occur.

13. **Share your good intention:** Explain why you are saying what you are. Example: "I want to be respectful of your ideas, Mrs. Smith— I want you to know that I do care what you think and feel."

This is another very safe and excellent option, one that requires nothing more than awareness of one's true motivation. Too often, people get trapped in arguments in which justifications, explanations, and defensiveness are bantered back and forth, with very little being gained and with tempers often rising. Teams can usually break or avoid such a cycle very easily just by sharing the good intention, which is usually a very honorable one. All a person has to know is what he or she was trying to accomplish with that thought, that line of reasoning, that statement or question. The tone of voice and the sincerity that are communicated will also be very important, of course. Compare and contrast the following alternatives:

"I never said that!" versus "I'd like to clarify what I meant."

"What do you mean by that?" versus "I really want to understand your thoughts and feelings."

"Nobody's out to get you" versus "I really want to be on your side."

"You're taking all this too personally" versus "I want you to feel safe and respected."

Notice in all examples the use of "I" terms, which tends to intensify the message, as opposed to "we," which can often weaken the statement ("I care how you feel" as opposed to "We care how you feel.") Notice also that sharing the intention has a lot in common with both talking from the heart and pointing at self: All three demonstrate the power that lies in sharing real feelings and here/now wishes in "I" terms.

14. **Refocus:** Gently lead a participant back to the issue at hand. Example: "Could I ask you to summarize the key points we need to understand about this?"

Refocusing can be useful in a number of situations, such as when a participant seems to be rambling or when any of the team members seem to be lost. It can also be a way of guiding the group out of unproductive topics and back into more productive ones (such as away from accusations or past history and into present concerns and underlying interests).

The value of this option is that it shows interest and openness and thus avoids the inherent risks of some of the less commendable alternatives. Instead of "You seem to be off track right now," or "We are running out of time," or "Can you stop blaming and bringing up the past?" a team member can accomplish the same good intention by gently refocusing. Such refocusing can be strengthened by incorporating some other options, as well, such as pointing at self, affirming, and returning to the good intention. Here is an example of such a blended response:

Mr. Smith, <u>I am having a little trouble,</u> [pointing at self]
and yet I really <u>want to follow</u> the [sharing good intention]
<u>many good points</u> you are raising. [affirming]
<u>Can you summarize</u> the key points [refocusing]
you want us to see?

15. **Use humor:** Use a joke or silliness to lower intensity (being careful not to appear to be disrespectful of anyone's feelings or ideas). Example: "My wife must have given me decaf this morning because I'm having a little trouble keeping up. Can you run that by me one more time?"

There's a funny thing about humor, and that is that some of us are much better at it than others. I can't tell you why that is, but I have noticed all my life how some people are just naturals at being able to say and get away with things that others of us can't, won't, or simply wouldn't dare.

I remember a wonderful example of humor being used to defuse a situation when I worked in juvenile corrections many years ago. A teenage student came up to her teacher at the end of a class and demanded that the teacher punch her point card (part of a reward system for good behavior). The student ended her demand with a threat, saying, "If you don't, I'm gonna knock your teeth in."

I was horrified and fully expected the teacher to respond with a stern reprimand or even a punishment. This teacher was no new kid on the block—she had been working with adolescents for more years than I (at that time) had been on this fine earth. She was also a very heavy-set woman, shaped more like a bowling ball than anyone I had ever met. This figured very much in the response she chose to make. When the student said, "I'm gonna knock your teeth in," she jokingly replied, "I wish somebody would. Then maybe I wouldn't eat so much!"

I would call this a classic example of using humor to sidetrack a potentially intense situation, one that could have led to serious consequences for the student. The wisdom of using humor in this case depended very much on discernment—knowing when it would or would not be appropriate—and having the kind of personality that could use it and get away with it.

Using humor is mentioned because it can be helpful. It does carry certain risks that make it best reserved for those who have the good judgment to use it only when it really would help. Nobody likes to be made fun of or to have their thoughts, feelings, or behavior ridiculed, especially in front of others. So if team members are going to use humor, they safeguard this option greatly by doing as that teacher did and poking fun only at themselves.

16. **Apologize:** Recognize a possible wrongdoing, even when it may not be your fault. Example: "I am really sorry if I've led you to think that we're not interested in Johnny's progress. I apologize for whatever I may have done to give that impression."

Note that the speaker is not apologizing "that you feel that way" or "that you think that way." Instead, it is for whatever *the speaker* may have done. This is an important point, and it is worth considering how much an apology can be negated when it is displaced from what I did to what you did. Contrast the following:

1. I am really sorry for whatever I may have done to upset you.

    I am really sorry that you feel upset.

2. I apologize if I said anything that seemed disrespectful.

    I apologize if you see me as disrespectful.

3. I am sorry if I was impolite.

    I am sorry you see me as impolite.

We can weaken an apology in other ways, as well.
A very meaningful saying is
Never ruin an apology with an excuse.
—Kimberly Johnson

Following any apology with a "but" runs the risk of striking through whatever was said that precedes it. As an example, consider, "I am really sorry to be late, but the phone rang just as I was heading out the door." Even without the *but,* the excuse can still weaken the effect: "I am really sorry to be late. The phone rang just as I was heading out the door." How much different does it sound when it includes no excuse at all: "I am really sorry to be late." Period.

An apology is only meaningful when it is sincere and when it shows an honest recognition of responsibility. Compare these alternatives and consider how they sound as they become progressively more accepting of responsibility:

- I am really sorry if you think I am disrespectful.

- I am really sorry if anything I did seemed to you to be disrespectful.

- I am really sorry if I seemed to be disrespectful.

- I am really sorry if I said or did anything that seemed disrespectful.

- I am really sorry if I said or did anything disrespectful.

- I am really sorry for being disrespectful.

It is interesting that, when people are asked what they really want in an argument or conflict, and even in a formal complaint or lawsuit, it can sometimes be nothing more than a simple recognition and an honest apology. It costs so little and can mean so very much.

17. **Ask for help:** Ask the person to tell you what he or she needs. Example: "Mrs. Jones, would you like to talk about your feel-

ings, or maybe take a break, or something else? What would be most helpful to you right now?"

While this option may need no explanation, there is at least one point that should be made. As I observe people trying to be helpful to others, I notice that they are often quick to *assume* what would be helpful and to decide and tell, rather than to ask and decide *together*. Thus, for example, they may suggest the group takes a break if someone seems angry, or they quickly move on to a different topic if someone shows tears and seems upset. With best of intentions, they have unilaterally made a decision they assume will be helpful without ever asking the person they are trying to help! In most cases, people make much wiser decisions, while communicating a great deal of caring and respect, just by including those they want to help and simply asking them. Making decisions independently always carries the risk of *not* being helpful, despite the best of intentions. As an example, I may decide that we should take a break to give you a chance to relax and not feel on the spot, but you see me as ignoring your feelings and avoiding having to consider your ideas. When in doubt, we can "check it out," as is discussed in option 18.

18. **When in doubt, check it out:** If a possible situation warrants confirmation, ask. Example: "Mr. Doe, are you maybe a little upset with me or something that was said?"

This very simple option serves at least two purposes, one of which may not be immediately obvious. First, of course, is that it can help to clarify thoughts or feelings that might otherwise remain ambiguous or hidden. The less obvious role it can play is to mirror to participants what is being perceived, which, if true, can now be moved from implicit to explicit. In other words, if a person checks out an assumption and it is *not* true, both people benefit from clarifying what the truth really is. On the other hand, if it is true, then that thought, feeling, or issue can be brought out into the open where it can be explored and either incorporated into the decision-making process or resolved so as not to pose an obstacle. A couple of illustrations may be helpful.

Chairperson: "Mr. Jones, I notice that you have been very quiet, and I wonder if you might be unhappy with anyone or with anything that was said today?"

Mr. Jones: "No, I'm not unhappy. I had to work really late last night and have had a touch of the flu or something, so I am just not really with it today. Sorry if I seem not to be involved or not my usual self."

In the above example, unless the unclear is brought out in the open, there is a possibility of misperceptions and emotional reactions from such assumptions as "He's really mad at me," or "He's just upset because we didn't follow his idea," or any such negative interpretations. By checking it out, the team can clarify the truth and move on in renewed cooperation.

But what if the negative perceptions *are* true? Here is a second and very different example:

Chairperson: "Mr. Jones, I notice that you have been very quiet, and I wonder if you might be unhappy with anyone or with anything that was said today?"

Mr. Jones: "Well, as long as you're asking, you all are going to do whatever you want to do no matter what I say, so I might as well just shut up and listen."

This second example begins exactly the same way: by checking out the assumption to see if it is true. Unlike in the first example, however, it is indeed true. The good news is that the team can now raise the unspoken negativity into open discussion and hopefully resolve it. The implicit has been made explicit, which allows it for the first time to be explored, understood, and hopefully put to rest. This exploration can take the form of a variety of the options that have been discussed. Some excellent responses might include any of the following:

• Say some more about that. {holding a focus}

- I am really sorry if I said anything to give that impression. [apology]

- I really do want you to share your thoughts and have an equal say in the decision. [sharing good intention]

- How can we best be helpful? [asking for help]

19. **Acknowledge:** Recognize a possible situation, feeling, or thought. Example: "Mrs. Jones, if I were you, I might feel really lost at this point because we have really covered a lot of ground this morning."

What better way to show that a listener really does understand than by supportively expressing the feelings *the other person* has? Doing so as a possibility rather than a certainty leaves an open door if, for whatever reason, the person does not want his or her feelings acknowledged (e.g., "No, I'm not feeling lost. I just don't understand what you are trying to say"). Such an open door can also be valuable if the perception is actually incorrect, in that it provides an easy opportunity to clarify the truth (e.g., "No, I'm not feeling lost. I'm just feeling a little overwhelmed with so much information and need a moment to digest each of those points").

Notice also how, in acknowledging, a cushion of safety is provided by using "I" terms and thus pointing at self ("If I were you, I might be feeling . . ."). Questions versus statements provide an additional safety net (checking it out by adding, "Am I right?" or "Am I off track?"). As mentioned before, some people are not comfortable getting close to their feelings or being asked to share their feelings in a group. On the other hand, some people are just the opposite and would really appreciate the caring shown and the opportunity to share. There is thus a much greater risk in saying (even if true), "You look absolutely horrified and must be just devastated by such a discouraging report," in contrast to "If I were you, I might be feeling kind of surprised or maybe even a little upset. Am I off track?"

20. **Shift to a comfort zone:** Focus on a topic that is easier to discuss or on another agenda item, and return to the more difficult topic later in the meeting. Example: "Mrs. Jones, what are some of the areas where you see Johnny really progressing these days? I've seen some big improvements in his temper control."

It is important to maintain a healthy balance of critical and complimentary remarks. Too much of the negative can obviously set an unpleasant and discouraging tone. Teams generally promote a positive tone by having a forward rather than a past-oriented outlook and by emphasizing what can be done or what has been achieved, rather than what can not or has not. While team members should always strive to be as positive and diplomatic as possible, there may be times when a shift to a different topic can provide a helpful break from disappointing or unpleasant news. It is a matter of timing and not one of denying or avoiding. The bypassed topic will and perhaps even must be revisited and addressed and certainly not ignored.

21. **Remind people of the ground rules:** Reflect agreements made earlier in the meeting. Example: "Team, I notice that some of us are leaving the room or talking on our cell phones. Am I wrong that we agreed to stay together and minimize distractions?"

Obviously, the members cannot refer to agreements made earlier if they didn't make any! And how valuable it can be to have such ground rules to fall back on when needed. This is one specific way in which conflict can be minimized by a well-planned and well-run meeting. As the old saying goes, "An ounce of prevention is worth a pound of cure." (Stage-setting and ground rules are covered in detail in Chapter 2.)

22. **Play with the time shape:** Propose a short-term solution that will be reevaluated later. Example: "Would you be willing to try this idea for 1 month and then reevaluate and maybe change it at our next meeting?"

This wonderful option can build bridges across many an impasse for the simple reason that people are much more likely to agree to something temporary rather than permanent, and most can see the wisdom of a trial period followed by a reevaluation. In fact, in Western cultures, people play with the time shape all the time—whenever a person rents an apartment with a lease, buys a car with a loan or a house with a mortgage, agrees to a 30-day trial membership, or subscribes to a magazine with annual renewal. In each of these examples, the buyer has a chance to consider the terms of a payment plan ("the time shape of money") or has a chance to back out if he or she doesn't like what they get. In the IEP environment, a possible deal, so to speak, may be sunk only because it is couched as all or nothing. Such either/or proposals may involve whether or not to remove a child from the classroom, whether or not to buy a laptop, whether or not to provide additional testing, and similar choices for the team to consider. In many cases, when dissension, resistance, and uncertainty are present, consensus can be greatly promoted just by changing the terms of the agreement.

Few people would buy a car at $20,000 cash on the barrelhead, and even fewer would (or could) buy a house with cash. And how many would take out a life membership in a country club they had never seen before? But most people would much more readily agree to 10% down and $1,000 per month for the house or a 30-day trial with no obligation for the country club. Both of these are playing with the time shape of a proposal. It can often be of enormous help in the IEP environment, as well. As examples

- How about if we do a behavioral assessment, and then decide if Bobby's spitting in class can be addressed without removing him?

- What if we ask the principal to look into the issue with the teacher, and then see if taking it to a higher authority is still necessary?

- How about if we arrange for Mary to try an AlphaSmart keyboard for a few weeks and then see if a laptop still seems necessary?

"How about" questions and "what if" possibilities are excellent ways to promote collaboration while at the same time demonstrating the affirming nature of asking questions.

23. **Make a deal:** Ask the other person to agree to speak up if he or she perceives a certain behavior or has a negative feeling. Example: "If you see me taking sides or if you at any point feel discounted, would you be willing to speak up and let me know?"

There is a certain amount of overlap between making a deal and some of the other intervention options, especially the previous one of playing with the time shape. Yet it has some other applications that make it unique. Making a deal can be especially useful for addressing negative or faulty perceptions, such as "You don't care what I think," "You only care about the money," "You just don't like him," and any of a long list of such allegations. The immediate tendency is often to deny, defend, and discount them with such responses as "No, we don't," "That's not true," "Yes, we do," "Let me explain," and similar games of tug-of-war. A helpful option that does not involve tugging is to firmly agree with the *interest* being highlighted and then make an agreement about what will happen the next time (if there is a next time) that it is perceived. For example, "I absolutely agree that we should not make decisions based on whether we like or don't like a child. I absolutely agree that money should not be our controlling factor. You are so right that your opinion should be heard and is important." *And then . . .*

- Would you be willing to tell me when you see me being uncaring about the child?

- Can you help us see it when we are being governed by money, if you see that happening?

- Would you point it out to us if at any time you feel ignored or discounted?

This option of making a deal involves making the implicit explicit by bringing out into the open the perceptions and feelings that might otherwise be hidden, while at the same time giving the dissatisfied team member some control over the perceived process. Only by bringing such perceptions out in the open can they be directly explored, understood, and resolved so that they no longer serve as obstructions to the harmony and real partnership of the team.

24. **Call security:** If at any time you really believe the safety of a participant is in jeopardy, err on the side of caution.

Obviously, this option is one that will rarely, if ever, be required. Yet, it is absolutely essential that every IEP team has such an option in place and knows how to use it. A question I love to ask at workshops is "How many of you know what your school's emergency procedures are? If you had someone suddenly turn violent at an IEP meeting, would you know what to do?" If the participants don't have a clear and meaningful answer, I give them the homework assignment of going to find out. Perish the thought that a team should ever have to use it, but at the same time, it is absolutely imperative to make sure that the protection of a security policy is in place.

25. **Suspend and reconvene:** If the meeting cannot proceed for legal reasons (e.g., because a required participant is not present) or because collaboration does not seem possible today (e.g., tempers are too high or adequate preparation was not done), terminating the meeting may be necessary. [This should be used only when truly necessary and when a legal time limit will not be crossed.]

Suspending a meeting is another option that should very rarely have to be used. It usually requires a great deal of preparing, clearing schedules, covering classes, and perhaps traveling, for all members of the IEP team to gather together under the same roof at the same time. Suspending and reconvening is sure to inconvenience one or more of the members, weaken team spirit, and set negative expectations for the future. If nothing else, it is far from an efficient use of time. The best protection against the need for such a circumstance is, of course, prevention—making sure all team members know when and where the meeting will be, what will be expected of them, and so on. In the event of an unforeseen development (a flat tire en route, an illness or family emergency), the importance of notifying the other members as soon as possible is, of course, self-evident.

A few notes are worth considering. Sometimes the choice to terminate a meeting may be made when not really necessary. For example, perhaps some testing was not completed. Before suspending and reconvening, however, the members can discuss whether the test results are really necessary for the meeting. Is the same information available from other sources? Are there other important topics that *can* be addressed while the team is assembled? If so, these topics can be covered today, thereby lightening the workload if another meeting does have to be scheduled.

Another question involves whether or not terminating the meeting is the best of all options. For example, one of the team members may be getting upset, perhaps tearful or enraged. It is important that the meeting not be terminated for the wrong reasons— just because the other members are uncomfortable with tears or anger or are uncertain about how best to proceed. It may be that taking a break, shifting to a comfort zone, asking for help, reminding people of the ground rules, or any of a variety of other options may be used with good results so that termination does not really become necessary. Furthermore, if at all possible, the decision should be made jointly—as a *group* decision. In this regard, if I (as chairperson) am thinking that this meeting should be terminated, I could tell the group or I could *ask* the group. A fundamental value underlying this approach is that decisions that affect the team as a whole should be made *together.* In this example, I could say, "Team, I am not sure that we can proceed together today without [that test report, or that teacher present, or that information, or with tempers so high]. What do you all think? Might it be better to suspend this meeting and come back together next month?" Asking is affirming. Aren't two heads usually better than one?

The list of 25 intervention options is presented in summary form on the following pages.

25 Intervention Options

1. **Share the conflict:** Express your own feelings and trust that the next steps will become clear. Example: "I feel kind of attacked right now. I'm not sure how to proceed."

2. **Hold a focus:** Ask for more at least twice, then ask to respond. Example: "Is there anything else you'd like to say? [Allow a response.] Anything else I should understand about this? [Allow a response.] May I respond to what you've said?"

3. **Paraphrase and reflect:** Simply repeat back what you are hearing. Example: "Let me see if I understand what you're saying. You think Sally's classroom teacher is really unfair and the school is not really giving your daughter the quality of education we're required to give?"

4. **Educate:** Give explanations, perhaps about policies, laws, and so on. Example: "We cannot transfer children to other schools unless their needs really cannot be met where they currently are."

5. **Confront the individual:** Objectively point out a person's disturbing behavior. Example: "Sally, I notice that you are raising your voice right now."

6. **Confront the group:** Make comments about the group rather than the individual. Example: "Are we clearly on task right now?"

7. **Reflect/invite to the group:** Share an observation and ask the group to assist. Example: "We seem to be kind of quiet right now. Any ideas how we might move through this?"

8. **Take a break:** A short break can provide time for tempers to cool. Example: "I wonder if a 5-minute leg stretch might be a good idea right now."

9. **Caucus:** Provide time for small-group or individual discussion. Example: "Mrs. Jones, would it be helpful to take a little time for just you and me to talk in private?"

10. **Probe for underlying interests:** Explore reasons so as to gain understanding. Example: "This issue seems to be very important to you, and you must have good reasons. Can you help us understand your thoughts about that?"

11. **Affirm:** Use praise as a means of support (perhaps along with another technique). Example: "I think you've raised some valid concerns there."

12. **Point at self:** Let any perceived ignorance, impatience, and so on be directed at you to avoid putting anyone else in an uncomfortable position. Example: "I'm not sure I am following you, Mrs. Jones. Could you rephrase that for me, please?"

13. **Share your good intention:** Explain why you are saying what you are. Example: "I really want to be respectful of your ideas, Mrs. Smith—I want you to know that I do care what you think and feel."

14. **Refocus:** Gently lead a participant back to the issue at hand. Example: "Could I ask you to summarize the key points we need to understand about this?"

15. **Use humor:** Use a joke or silliness to lower intensity (being careful not to appear to be disrespectful of anyone's feelings or ideas). Example: "My wife must have given me decaf this morning because I'm having a little trouble keeping up. Can you run that by me one more time?"

16. **Apologize:** Recognize a possible wrongdoing, even when it may not be your fault. Example: "I am really sorry if I've led you to think that we're not interested in Johnny's progress. I apologize for whatever I may have done to give that impression."

17. **Ask for help:** Ask the person to tell you what he or she needs. Example: "Mrs. Jones, would you like to talk about your feelings, or maybe take a break, or something else? What would be most helpful to you right now?"

18. **When in doubt, check it out:** If a possible situation warrants confirmation, ask. Example: "Mr. Doe, are you maybe a little upset with me or something that was said?"

19. **Acknowledge:** Recognize a possible situation, feeling, or thought. Example: "Mrs. Jones, if I were you, I might feel really lost at this point because we have really covered a lot of ground this morning."

20. **Shift to a comfort zone:** Focus on a topic that is easier to discuss or on another agenda item, and return to the more difficult topic later in the meeting. Example: "Mrs. Jones, what are some of the areas where you see Johnny really progressing these days? I've seen some big improvements in his temper control."

21. **Remind people of the ground rules:** Reflect agreements made earlier in the meeting. Example: "Team, I notice that some of us are leaving the room or talking on our cell phones. Am I wrong that we agreed to stay together and minimize distractions?"

22. **Play with the time shape:** Propose a short-term solution that will be reevaluated later. Example: "Would you be willing to try this idea for 1 month and then reevaluate and maybe change it at our next meeting?"

23. **Make a deal:** Ask the other person to agree to speak up if he or she perceives a certain behavior or has a negative feeling. Example: "If you see me taking sides or if you at any point feel discounted, would you be willing to speak up and let me know?"

24. **Call security:** If at any time you really believe the safety of a participant is in jeopardy, err on the side of caution.

25. **Suspend and reconvene:** If the meeting cannot proceed for legal reasons (e.g., because a required participant is not present) or because collaboration does not seem possible today (e.g., tempers are too high or adequate preparation was not done), terminating the meeting may be necessary. (This should be used only when truly necessary and when a legal time limit will not be crossed.)

Chapter 8

The Wisdom
to Know

T he third corner of the triad of conflict resolution is, of course, "the wisdom to know the difference." When it comes to preventing and resolving conflict in the IEP environment, the issue of wisdom has a number of applications. All relate to decision making—what to do, when to do it, and why. This chapter approaches the decision-making process from several perspectives:

1. When to intervene as opposed to just accept

2. How to make decisions from an inner "ring of truth"

3. How to improve the system as a whole

4. How to monitor team satisfaction, both individually and collectively

THE ISSUE OF ACCEPTANCE

When should IEP team members accept that they have no power in a particular situation and that it is best to just take a deep breath, think positively, and let it "roll off their backs" like the proverbial water off a duck? There are many seemingly wise remarks that are made in relation to IEP issues:

Accept your limitations. There's only so much you can do.

With people like that [parents, administrators, staff members, students], you really can't expect too much.

We need to be realistic and understand that ideals can't always be met.

We can't be expected to do it their way when they don't give us the money, the training, or the time to do it.

The people who made these rules are lawyers and politicians, not teachers.

Lighten up: You take this far too seriously.

IEP meetings are designed by people with a 6:1 student–teacher ratio; I have 23 in my class.

When was the last time he [the author] was in an IEP meeting?

I have a heard a wide variety of such comments by now, and they form an interesting picture when assembled all in one place at the same time. For one thing, they usually reflect the negative projections of the naysayers; instead of possibility thinking, they reflect impossibility thinking (and what we expect, we tend to get). Second, they relieve the speaker of responsibility: "I can't be expected to live the vision of the IEP team because he, she, and they didn't do this, that, or the other." In addition, they serve as sweeping generalizations that give a reason for broadly discounting what is being offered: If lawyers and politicians made the rules, the rules are not relevant, appropriate, or realistic for educators. And yet is there no merit to such remarks—at least sometimes? How can anyone really know in a given IEP situation whether it's time to kick and splash—like the optimistic frog in Chapter 4—or time, instead, to kick back, let go, and just relax?

Whenever people are faced with a challenging situation, whether in the IEP environment or anywhere, they will always have to decide whether to intervene or just to let it slide. The fact is that decision making is a universal feature of being alive, and we are all making decisions every moment of our lives. However, many of these decisions are made so automatically and subconsciously that we do not see the decision-making process that is at work. (Should I tie my right shoe first or my left shoe first? Should I park in this space or that one? Should I say something now or just keep my opinions to myself? Should I read another few pages or just go to sleep?) The decision-making process in conflict situations is not fundamentally different. What *is* different is only the unpleasant feelings that are present and the choice to oppose (the two defining hallmarks of conflict). With awareness comes the ability to make "flexible choices," and team members benefit from raising their awareness of the decisions that *are* being made, as well as the options available to them.

FOUR CONSIDERATIONS FOR INTERVENTION

When it comes to conflict intervention in almost any situation, there are four factors worth including in the decision-making process:

- Frequency

- Duration

- Intensity

- Impact

Frequency, of course, refers to how often a particular circumstance arises. Imagine that one of your IEP team members is late for a meeting. Is this the first time it has happened, and is it something that resulted from unusual circumstances? Do you have reason to think it will happen again? If this member is usually or always late, this may be a good reason to find the courage to change this problematic situation, as opposed to adopting the serenity to let it go. The decision to just accept it, perhaps in saying "lighten up and don't make waves," is sure to result in a high probability of the chronic lateness continuing with similar or even increasing frequency.

Similar logic can be applied to decisions the team must make for other kinds of challenges, as well. When developing IEPs, the team must often make its decisions based on frequency. Are the student's low test scores typical or exceptional? Is the unruly classroom behavior a one-time occurrence or is it often repeated? Is the child's absenteeism common or only occasional? Obviously, the answers to such questions of frequency will have everything to do with the decisions the team will make.

The second decisive element to consider is duration: How long-lasting is the challenging situation? This question can be closely related to frequency or completely independent of it. For example, it may be that an administrator only takes one cell phone call in an entire meeting, but the call lasts for 20 minutes. An unhappy parent may walk away mad just one time but does not attend another IEP meeting for 2 years. The student may be absent only once in a school term but is gone for 3 weeks at a time. In any of these examples, the frequency may be acceptable; the *duration* is what makes the issue such a problem.

The third consideration is intensity. When a teacher responds to her approach being questioned, is there a hint of defensiveness that many would not even notice or a sharpness so strong that it cannot be missed? When the parents hear some disappointing news, do they sigh deeply and avert their eyes for a moment or break down with inconsolable tears? When an administrator expresses concern about something that wasn't done, does he become slightly irritated or purple with rage? Obviously, behaviors of very mild intensity can easily be overlooked (not that they necessarily *should* be), but it becomes much more difficult to overlook them when they are really loud and clear.

Finally, and certainly the most decisive of all when it comes to decision making about conflict, what is the impact of the issue in question? Very often it is not so much the frequency, duration, or even intensity that makes it necessary to intervene but rather the implications for the work of the team. In fact, one can have behaviors that are of very low frequency, duration, and intensity that are still of such impact that they *must* be addressed. As examples, a student may have only one time, for just a brief moment, very quietly pulled a knife on the playground—minimal frequency, brief duration, low intensity, but huge potential impact. A parent may have only once, very succinctly and softly, called the teacher and all of his ancestors a bunch of blankety-blanks, but the bombshell dropped on the IEP meeting may have been colossal—and for several years to come.

When it comes to impact, remembering the vision of the IEP team can make it easier to decide whether a given situation warrants intervention. That vision is clear: to work in partnership to develop the best IEP for the particular child. Anything that threatens this ability is something that must be resolved. Team members cannot ethically simply lighten up and accept their limitations when a child is getting short changed. Team members cannot responsibly just adopt serenity by breathing deep, tapping into their inner peace, and holding positive images of beaches in the Bahamas. They must, instead, get tough, get busy, and find the courage and skills they'll need to effectively intervene.

DECISION-MAKING TECHNIQUES

But what if it isn't so cut and dried? Maybe I don't really know whether I should talk to Mr. Mann about his diplomacy at IEP meetings. What if Mrs. Doe's denial is just part of who she is and doesn't need to be made into an issue? Maybe it isn't clear whether Freddie's behavior might lead to a bad situation that could have been prevented. But what if we make a big mistake that we will seriously regret one day? How can teams ever be sure? Where can they find the wisdom to decide?

As mentioned before, decision making is something all of us are doing all of the time, every day of our lives. And with each decision comes, inherently, the risk that the decision we make will be wrong or at least not the best. Many decisions are absolutely harmless. If I decide to tie my right shoe before my left or instead decide to tie my left before my right, well, probably no harm done either way. But not all decisions are so free of significant consequences, and as a basic and inevitable fact of life, there is no such thing as *not* deciding. To not decide is itself a decision: to *avoid* deciding, or to let someone else decide, or to just do whatever I do unconsciously out of habit. Because many IEP decisions do involve some element of risk, the question becomes more than academic: How can teams guard against the risk of mistakes and make the wisest decisions that they can?

Although it may be very easy to agree that the purpose of the team is to do whatever is best for the child, it is not always so easy to be sure what that would look like in a particular situation. This does not mean, however, that there is no way to find out. Here are some suggestions.

Talk, Talk, Talk

There is a definite power and even magic that comes from discussion in a safe and respectful atmosphere. By sharing feelings, thoughts, and experiences with others, a path forward that all can support usually emerges. The first recommendation for decision making, therefore, is don't go it alone: Talk with the others involved, seek out people with more knowledge or experience, and talk privately if the topic may be sensitive. You can even talk to yourself!

People generally make their decisions based on a hard-to-explain inner feeling of rightness. They get a "ring of truth" that doing this or that would be good, while the alternatives don't seem to line up as well. "Trust your gut. Follow your bliss. Listen to your heart. Go with the flow." All of these are familiar phrases that speak to this inner feeling of rightness. When I raise this issue with groups, most people report that when they trust that inner feeling, it usually works out very well. Conversely, when they think back to times when they did *not* follow it, they usually wish later that they had.

Looking to others as a sounding board and an opportunity to bounce ideas can very much help to clarify what that inner feeling of rightness really is. This is especially true when people sincerely *want* to do what is right—not what is easy, not what is most popular, not what is most comfortable or familiar, but what is really best for the child. Because of the value of clarifying thoughts and feelings—and actually verbalizing them aloud—the following technique can be very helpful. It is usually something to be done privately in preparation for a meeting, rather than during the meeting itself (although this need not be an absolute rule). The exercise below can be done with a trusted friend or alone, but it should be done aloud. Its applications are limitless.

Two–Chair Exercises

1. Take the issue and divide it into two or more alternatives—the pro side and the con side; for example, I should (pro) or should not (con) recommend removing Freddie from the classroom.

2. Assume a comfortable position in a chair, and speak from only one of the two positions. State the premise and give all the reasons and feelings behind that position. ("I know it is right to remove Freddie from the general classroom, and here's why . . . .")

3. When you are finished, listen within to how comfortable and right that position feels. It can be helpful to give yourself a score on a scale of 1–10, with 10 meaning completely right.

4. Proceed to a second chair and repeat from the other position. ("I know that it is *not* right to remove Freddie from the general classroom because . . . .")

5. Repeat and dialogue between the two chairs until you have a sense of what really does feel most right to you. That is, move

back and forth from one chair to the other and respond aloud to the reasons being presented from each position.

Usually a little time spent arguing with yourself and exploring the different perspectives will soon clarify what really does feel right and why. However, if the answer remains unclear, just respect your uncertainty and be willing to let it be for a little while. It could mean that the time to decide has not yet arrived or that there are pieces of the puzzle that you don't yet have but which will usually become clear with just a little time.

Another possible obstacle in using two-chair exercises is that fears and preconceptions can be getting in the way. When this happens, their inner "yeah, buts" may be keeping people from being able to honestly explore their options so that they really can find their inner sense of rightness. The solution, however, is simple if they lead with the sincere desire to explore their options and find out what really is right for them, and if they identify what their fears and preconceptions actually are. When people are aware of their fears and preconceptions, they can then, in a sense, set them aside for a moment while they do the exercise. Let's look at an example.

Suppose I, as principal, think that removing Freddie from the classroom may be best, but I am not really sure. As I sincerely open myself to the truth of the matter and observe my mental pictures, I can begin to see and hear my "yeah, buts." I imagine (and feel sure) that his parents would hit the ceiling. I also picture the superintendent questioning my judgment, especially when he gets angry notes from the parents or other school staff. So far so good: I can now identify my preconceptions as to what I see happening if I make the recommendation that Freddie be removed from the classroom. I can also identify my fears as I picture the superintendent asking for my resignation after 15 happy years with the district.

Now that I am aware of my thoughts and feelings, I can set them aside, almost like putting them in the corner for a moment, while I continue to work with the two-chair exercise. I can always call them back to myself at any time that I want to. Here's what this example might look like in a sample dialogue between my pro and con chairs:

Pro: I know it is right to remove Freddie from the general class-room, and here's why. His behavior is unpredictable and sometimes very severe. We did an assessment last term and know that his emotions can get the better of him, especially when he gets frustrated. As he gets older and bigger, the ef-fect on the other children gets more pronounced, and the teacher does not have the extra assistant she had last year. So I know we need to move him. [Score for rightness: 6]

Con: I know it is *not* right to remove Freddie from the general class-room, and here's why. Freddie is very likable and is trying hard to do his best. He could be put on another medication that might help him stay more relaxed and in control. The teacher could get some coaching in how to handle him, and the par-ents can do some frustration-control work with him at home. So I am sure he should remain in the classroom. [Score: 4]

Pro: It is not about liking him, it's about what's best for his edu-cation. We don't know what other medications are available or even whether they would help. If they do, we can always move him back in the future. It's not fair to add to the teacher's or parents' responsibilities, nor can we be sure that their extra efforts would be enough. We can not leave him where he is. [5]

Con: It *is* the responsibility of the parents and teacher, and trying to move him back after a time in a separate setting is really hard on everyone. So he should stay. [4]

Pro: If Freddie hits or bites another child just one more time, there could be some really serious problems for all involved, and we have no reason to think his self-control has improved all that much. It is too great a risk at this time. He should be removed. [8]

Con: I could lose my job if the parent complains to the superintendent. So I know he should stay. [4]

Pro: I don't have to present removing him as a decision—only as an option for the group to consider. I can give my reasons for thinking it *may* be necessary. If it is a group decision, I wouldn't be punished. All things considered, I can recommend he be removed but not decide that he should be. [10— full feeling of rightness]

Con: Okay.

Note that by setting aside fears and preconceptions, I can just do the exercise and see where it leads me. As I consider the different options, I may see that new and unexpected aspects of the issue come to the surface, perhaps some I hadn't thought of before. Also, what often happens is that the dialoguing process leads to a different way of phrasing the premise (in this example, from "I should make a decision" to "I can present it as an option").

Before moving on, it may be helpful to list a few other specific examples where decision making could be assisted by using two-chair exercises. Consider the following, among an endless list of possibilities for any of the members in the IEP setting:

- The decision to confront a team member with being late or unprepared

- The decision to address a team member's negative or defensive attitude

- The decision to request a more suitable meeting time and place

- The decision to suspend a meeting if a member becomes rude and hostile

- The decision to apologize to a hostile parent

- The decision to ask an administrator for more support or training

Two-chair exercises can often be a helpful and even powerful means to "try it on for size" and so find the wisdom that is needed for a difficult decision. Try it. You'll like it.

SYSTEM SUGGESTIONS

The Introduction to this book includes a summary of the parent concerns that underlie many of the conflicts that arise in the IEP environment. If conflict prevention and resolution is to be achieved, these concerns must obviously be explored and meaningfully addressed. At the same time, however, the parent members of the team represent only one or two seats at the table. In the discussion of principled negotiation in Chapter 3, some of the people issues were presented that relate to the *other* seats. It was emphasized that the feelings, pressures, responsibilities, and limitations of the staff members are also significant considerations. How they respond to and manage these issues will figure greatly in the overall effectiveness and harmony of the team.

Asking school personnel to share their thoughts about how the IEP environment can be improved has been just as enlightening as asking parents. Not only can it be helpful for a deeper understanding but it also underscores the importance of a *systemwide* approach to conflict prevention and resolution if the vision of true partnership is to be achieved. Typical suggestions of school personnel can be grouped into four distinct though interrelated categories:

1. Cooperation among participants

2. Support of participants

3. Training of participants

4. Workload issues

What follows is a summary of what IEP team leaders have shared with me as to what is most needed to improve the system as a whole.

Cooperation Among Participants

1. Members must be on time and prepared for meetings, recognizing that the entire team is dependent on the professionalism of its members.

2. Members must treat one another with respect. Attitude is critically important in any endeavor, and an atmosphere of mutual respect is vital.

3. Members must follow through on commitments made at IEP meetings. No one member can ensure the success of the team, and each member must make it a priority to fulfill his or her responsibilities.

Support of Participants

4. School administrators must support teachers being out of their classrooms for IEP meetings and assist in providing class coverage.

5. School administrators who are not there in person must support the decisions of the team. The team's decisions are made after review of many factors, and it is unreasonable to designate a committee chair but then reject the decisions made. Similarly, the team must be supported in following the law and district policies and not just expected to do what the absent principal or another administrator wants done.

6. Accountability must be expected of all participants: principals and superintendents must help committee chairs ensure that team members fulfill their obligations. Without such assistance, the designated chair often has little authority and little recourse.

7. The chain of command must hold a similar vision of the importance, authority, and legal responsibilities of the IEP team. Principals need to have a clear understanding of the IEP environment so that they can provide appropriate guidance and leadership to school staff. Superintendents must recognize and ensure this knowledge base among the school administrators in their districts.

8. Administrators must support the provision of training for parents and school staff and not just for a limited few.

9. Clear job descriptions must be developed so that all school staff are aware of and understand their responsibilities to the IEP team.

10. Clear channels of resources must be provided for IEP team members to receive assistance when needed, as well as timely responses to legal and other IEP-related questions.

11. Routine evaluations should be done so that IEP teams have a means of measuring their effectiveness, satisfaction, and success.

Training of Participants

12. School administrators must receive training in how to chair IEP teams, as well as training in what can and should be expected of anyone they select as their designees.

13. General classroom teachers must receive training in IEP matters with periodic follow-up as laws, policies, and procedures change.

14. All team members must have a clear understanding of what an IEP meeting entails and what the legal responsibilities of the team are, as well as the responsibilities of each individual member.

15. New committee chairs would benefit from having mentors who are more experienced, as well as from periodic training programs in IEP-related topics.

16. Opportunities should be provided for committee chairs to discuss and perhaps role-play with other committee chairs some of the challenging situations they encounter.

17. Supervisors should assist staff who participate in IEP teams to develop professional growth plans that will enhance IEP team skills.

Workload Issues

18. A suitable meeting place should be provided so that teams can meet in a reasonably quiet and comfortable location that is free from distractions and interruptions.

19. Administrators must allow flex time, especially when staff must work long or unusual hours to accommodate the need of participants for evening or weekend meetings.

20. Administrators must help ensure an equitable workload distribution so that some school staff are not spending excessive amounts of time in IEP meetings and associated paperwork at the expense of other responsibilities. (This can often happen when there are many more eligible students at a particular school with fewer staff to serve them.)

21. Administrators should assist teams in developing an efficient method of paperwork, perhaps through updated technology and software, so as to ease the time demands that reporting can require.

22. Clear channels for funding should be developed so that IEP teams can efficiently follow through on the commitments they make and avoid resistance and arguments about who will cover what expenses.

The purpose of providing such a list is not to explore the suggestions in detail but only to present them for consideration. Awareness of these issues may encourage the further discussion that will help team members take whatever steps they deem most appropriate in their particular schools or districts. Such sharing of information can also increase the respect and understanding that team members have for each other and for the specific challenges the different members may bring to the meeting. This, in turn, can increase the mutual support, harmony, and effectiveness of IEP teams, both individually and in general.

MEASURING SUCCESS

As mentioned in the Introduction, most schools and districts have no mechanisms in place by which to assess the level of satisfaction among their IEP team members. All too often, the first signs of dissatisfaction take the form of empty chairs at the table, angry phone calls or letters, or requests for formal investigations or due process hearings. Because conflict is invariably fueled by unpleasant feelings, it only follows that early warning of dissatisfaction can go far toward resolving those bad feelings before they take the form of conflict and possibly escalate into expensive and unpleasant proceedings. What is also important is that early warning can allow teams to preserve their harmony, cooperation, and effectiveness before their team spirit erodes to the point that any semblance of partnership no longer exists. Without such assessment mechanisms in place, interventions are more likely to be curative rather than preventative. They may even be like the proverbial closing of the doors only *after* the horses have left the barn: By the time action is taken, a great deal of damage may already have been done. In the case of formal complaint investigations, due process hearings, and even mediation, this will so often be the case. In terms of "the wisdom to know the difference," routine assessment can play a vital role in giving teams the feedback they need to make wise and timely decisions.

Objectives of Assessment

Once it is understood how important it is to "keep a finger on the pulse" of IEP team satisfaction, the next question becomes how best teams can do this. The answer, however, can only follow from a clear idea of what it is they are trying to achieve. In other words, teams must first look at their *goals and objectives* for assessing the satisfaction of the team. A few of the most immediately apparent are:

1. To ensure that real partnership is achieved and maintained, so as to be in keeping with the intention of federal law

2. To maintain a strong *team* approach for the development of the best possible IEPs (through shared information and shared decision making) and to ensure the success of those IEPs through shared implementation

3. To minimize the frequency, duration, intensity, and impact of conflict through early awareness and prompt intervention

4. To reduce the enormous costs so often associated with formal complaints and due process hearings—in time, delays, dissatisfaction, stress, bitterness, damaged future relationships, and legal fees. The thousands of dollars, hundreds of hours, and incalculable emotional energy that each of these so often entails can surely be much better spent for the benefit of all involved, especially the children.

The costs of conflict can be very high. What options are available for preventative assessment, and what are the pros and cons of each?

Self-Report Inventories

As mentioned in the Introduction, those schools and districts that do use an assessment process often rely on written self-report inventories, which are prone to a number of significant drawbacks. Written evaluation forms hastily completed at the end of a meeting are likely to result in a positive and misleading picture. The probability of error is increased if those evaluation forms are taken from the meeting or sent to participants at a later time with the expectation that they will be returned by mail. Once again, a misleading and positive picture is likely, probably compounded by a very low response rate.

The pros of using written evaluation forms are that they are usually quick and easy to complete, and they can be uniform across the school, district, or other catchment area. If they *are* used, they should be short and easy to complete. They should require little time and only basic verbal skills, perhaps by involving the circling of numbers on a scale of 1 to 10 with spaces provided for recommendations or comments. A sample form is provided at the end of this chapter.

If using the self-report approach, it is important that participants understand its purpose and that they be encouraged to speak openly and honestly for the benefit of the team and the children. Obviously, if an evaluation becomes nothing more than a routine and empty exercise, it cannot be expected to have much value, and so it *must* be done in the spirit in which it is designed. Teams must also remember that they can never expect honesty unless they show a willingness to receive it—with respect and genuine openness. If the members are quick to become defensive or argumentative, they will quickly close the doors to genuine sharing in the future. The channels of communication *must* remain open, and the keys to effective communication (addressed in Chapter 4) are once again worth keeping in mind—holding a focus, talking from the heart, listening with respect, and maintaining the spirit of friendship.

Another very important consideration with regard to self-report inventories is that they must not be used in isolation. Instead, they can be used in conjunction with other approaches that can help to provide what the members are ultimately looking for: an early and accurate indication of their levels of effectiveness and team satisfaction.

State-Level Statistics

Most, if not all, states gather statistics concerning the number of due process hearing requests, formal complaints, and IEP-related mediations that are occurring, usually on an annual basis. There is some variation in how readily available these statistics are. (In some but not all states, this information can be accessed through the state department of education via the Internet or will be sent upon request.) There is also variation in the way these statistics are assembled and the degree of potential overlap between categories. For example, if a single formal complaint is unsuccessfully mediated and then evolves into a due process hearing, that same one incident may appear in all three categories, depending on how the statistics are compiled. A further complication is that the processes themselves are not uniform from one state to another. Who can serve as a hearing officer and what authority that officer has can vary greatly. Some states will not provide mediation of pending complaint investigations, while others permit mediation at any time it is requested. Some states mediate a good percentage of IEP-related conflicts, while others mediate very, very few.

Statewide statistics should certainly be kept and should be made public—for a number of reasons. With all their limitations, these numbers are still a good, *rough* indicator of the level of conflict within the special education system. They are especially useful to the extent that they show trends, especially if there is a sharp increase or decrease over time. The general public has an inherent right to such information from their tax-supported educational systems, and rough though such numbers may be, they can serve to temper other indicators. For example, a state or region that concludes it has little conflict and no reason to make changes but at the same time has a huge increase in the number of hearing requests over the last few years is clearly not looking at the facts. Conversely, such statistics can reveal improvement trends following conflict-reduction initiatives. As an example, if a district or region provides conflict-oriented training and then sees a significant reduction in complaints and hearing requests, it may be seeing confirmation that its teams are indeed making progress.

Yet another benefit of statewide statistics can be in highlighting the specific issues that are most often leading to conflict. If a state is seeing a sharp rise in the number of legal actions being brought in a particular area, greater education, funding, and/or staffing may be needed in that regard. For example, there may have been an increase in due process hearings over the alleged denial of free appropriate public education (FAPE) because school staff assigned to students are allegedly unqualified personnel. Perhaps they really *are* unqualified, and stricter hiring and certification policies are the answer. Or perhaps the personnel are sufficiently qualified, and IEP team participants would benefit from greater training in what really does or does not constitute the provision of FAPE when it comes to staff certifications and credentials.

The cons of using statewide statistics as an assessment tool are, as mentioned before, that these numbers are only very rough indicators that fail to consider a number of variables. For example, is a decrease in hearing requests due to a real decrease in dissatisfaction or, instead, to changing reporting methods or increased encouragement of settlements by the law firms that handle education issues? Is a significant *increase* in the number of IEP-related mediations a reflection of increased conflict or only of increased promotion of the use of this service? Another limitation of statistics is that they are so broad in scope (state- or region-wide) that they may be of little help to the individual district or school and even less help to the particular IEP team. With this limitation in mind, let's turn to some options that will be more helpful at the most immediate level.

Standard Agenda Topic: Feedback

A simple means of ending every IEP team meeting can be to include, as a standing agenda item, closing remarks and feedback. One form this can take is to simply go around the table and give everyone a chance to say whatever it is they would like to say by way of closure. The chairperson might lead with such questions as

- Before we end for today, would anyone like to share any thoughts or feelings he or she has not yet had a chance to share?

- How are we feeling about today's meeting? Any positives or negatives anyone would like to share, or any recommendations for our next meeting?

- Is there anything else anyone would like to say before we close for today?

As teams do this, it is important to be alert not just to the words but to some of the other indicators, such as body language, facial expressions, tones of voice, and even silence.

A follow up by phone a few days later can be very helpful whenever there is reason to suspect that someone may have left the meeting unhappy or ill at ease: "Mrs. Doe, I just wanted to touch base and see how you are feeling about our meeting the other day. I had a sense you were kind of unhappy about some things—can we talk about it?" Usually the caring and respect expressed through such a gesture will go far to alleviating any hard feelings before they do damage.

Informal Interviews

It is important not to overlook the obvious: If teams want to know what their members think, why not simply ask them? Interviewing can be done in a variety of ways. A committee chairperson can periodically and routinely phone each of the members of the IEP team to ask such questions as

- How do you think we are doing as a team?

- Are there any suggestions or concerns you might have?

- What would help us do better?

- Would you agree to let me know if at any time you are unhappy with a meeting?

Another form of periodic or routine interviewing can be done by one of the team members when there is an absent member (especially a parent). Questions might include

- Your presence is really important to me. Is there a particular reason you weren't able to attend our last meeting?

- How are you feeling about the team and its members?

- Are you feeling included and respected?

- Are we meeting at a time that is convenient for you?

Additional valuable interviews can include periodic discussions with leaders of parent organizations, such as parent resource centers, advocacy groups, and support groups. How are parents feeling, in general, about their involvement with schools? What concerns seem to be voiced most often? Any suggestions as to how parents and schools can work together more effectively? Maintaining open communication is *so* important, and any opportunity to share and work together in the spirit of common purpose and mutual respect is likely to pay big dividends.

Yet another possibility is to have an impartial third party do routine interviews of IEP team members, with the assurance of confidentiality unless otherwise agreed. For example, "Hi, I'm Bob White with the Utopian Independent Schools, and I am phoning IEP team members in the district to get some confidential feedback on how teams are doing, how people are feeling, and what kinds of questions, concerns, or recommendations they may have." Some readers may be quick to think in terms of "yeah, buts": "Yeah, but we're already much too busy to do that." "Yeah, but what if the people called don't want to talk?" "Yeah, but what if they just give a bunch of unfair negatives?" "Yeah, but there's nothing we could do about it anyway." Yeah, but *I* say hear it now or hear it in other ways.

That is, teams, schools, and districts can keep open the doors to communication or watch the negativity increase and come back in more expensive ways that are so often unnecessary and preventable—and more difficult to resolve. Furthermore, isn't it possible that much of the feedback that is received will be *positive* and will serve as powerful reinforcers to keep teams doing all the wonderful things they are doing right? Sometimes a simple "She was so understanding," or "He is such a good listener," or "They really care about my son and how we are doing," can go a long way to keeping spirits high. Sometimes it takes an interview to bring such positives out in the open and help teams to see what it is they should keep doing more of. School administrators, teachers, corporate executives, and business managers are all increasingly coming to see that "we get what we reward" and that positives in abundance are the best way of shaping desired and success-promoting behaviors.

A final note here: Having a third party contact IEP team members (especially the parent or student members) will probably warrant permission in advance. Yet any school or district choosing to use such an option can make up a simple release form that can be distributed to all IEP team members at the beginning of a school year, with signature clearly voluntary.

Periodic Conferences

A final recommendation is that time be made available for conferencing by stakeholders. In this regard, an open forum can be provided for airing, sharing, and making suggestions perhaps once or twice each year. As one option, this sharing might be done as a segment of an annual conference and presented to the participants as part of a *kaizen* process of continual improvement. Just as businesses and industries are always looking for ways to improve so as to maintain high customer satisfaction and a competitive edge, schools can do the same with regard to the very important work they do: partnering in the IEP environment. IEP teams, too, can continually strive to maintain the best possible product for the people they serve, so that a team can say, "No finer IEP can be found anywhere on the planet but right here, at our school, with us!"

RECOMMENDATIONS AND CONCLUSIONS

So of all these assessment options, which one is best? How can teams most easily get the greatest wisdom for their ongoing decision making? Well, when it comes to assessment options, why not do them all? The cost in time and expense of using every option described is probably far less than just one or two due process hearings, with none of the harmful side effects. If a team's, school's, or district's efforts to encourage open, honest, and frequent dialogue so as to increase team satisfaction while providing for early intervention in dissatisfactions—if such efforts can save just one due process hearing, they have probably more than paid for themselves. The payoff is not just in dollars but in harmony, efficiency, and success for all involved, especially the children.

IEP Meeting Evaluation Form

This evaluation form is intended to help us work more effectively together and to do our best possible work as a team for the benefit of our students. Thank you for caring enough to share your honest thoughts and feelings.

1. On a scale of 1–10, with 10 high, please indicate your overall satisfaction with today's meeting by circling one of the following:

   1 2 3 4 5 6 7 8 9 10

2. What did you find most worthwhile or commendable about this meeting?

3. How might this meeting have been improved? What might we do differently next time?

4. Any additional comments?

Chapter 9

Where We Go from Here

A t bedtime, I usually read a few pages from a book I have set aside for just that purpose. I enjoy this reading very much and have been doing it for years. However, if anyone were to ask me the next day or the next week what I read, I doubt I could possibly say. I may be very sure that I enjoyed the pages I read, and I may have an occasional recollection or two, but most of the time, my new information is gone with the wind—I can't remember a thing. And yet I know this in advance. I know that my bedtime reading is basically, and by design, nothing more than an enjoyable and relaxing activity before drifting off to meet the sandman. This may be well and good for purely recreational reading, but it would be a very different story if my IEP, or someone else's, depended on it.

So here we are near the end of a fairly elaborate book. By now, you have probably devoted a considerable amount of your valuable time and attention to the many topics that have been covered. In all probability, you have a sincere desire to strengthen your understanding of the IEP environment and to enhance your contribution as a valuable member of an important team. Would it be worthwhile, therefore, to devote a few pages to the issue of how a person can maximize the potential gains from the time and energy invested? Surely you would not want this book to be for you what my bedtime reading is for me!

If readers do, in fact, want to ensure their greatest gains, what can they do to create a bridge between the time spent here and the time spent in the IEP environment? The answer lies in the commitment the individual reader is willing to make on a personal level to connecting new reading to new skills—that is, to changing his or her IEP teamwork for the better.

Whatever the area of endeavor, growth occurs in three progressive stages: from the conceptual stage, to knowing, to living. Thus, whether in brick laying, opera singing, snow boarding, or finger painting, the novice comes first to perceive a new idea, then to fully understand that idea, and finally to demonstrate mastery of the new idea in behavioral expression. This process can be accelerated by first defining one's growing edges and then making a personal "action plan."

DEFINING GROWING EDGES

Chapter 1 presents the concept of growing edges and emphasizes that so long as we are alive, every single one of us without exception is growing. In different ways and at different rates, all human beings are taking their next steps forward on a lifelong journey of growth and learning. These steps, and the gains they reflect, will occur more quickly and will be more pronounced when people set a conscious direction and add some intentional effort. It is said that all people are the captains of their destinies. With such a metaphor in mind, if a person wants to sail downstream, he or she can do so more quickly and more effectively by not just floating down the river of life but by actively steering and paddling, thereby being all the more certain of getting wherever it is the person wants to go. This is as true in the IEP arena as in any other aspect of successful living.

The first step is thus to decide where team members, as individuals, really want to go—to set objectives on a personal level. This process of goal setting follows easily from defining one's growing edges. To do this, one need only think back to the many topics, insights, and techniques that have come into focus in the process of reading. A few moments spent in inner reflection and followed with pencil and paper can be very helpful. If this sounds worthwhile, why not take a few moments now to review the major topics covered and to look for whatever it might have been that particularly spoke to you. What stands out as something you'd like to understand more fully or explore in greater depth, or as a skill or technique that you would particularly like to master? A quick review of the table of contents and a skim reading of the headings within the chapters might be helpful in this regard. The purpose is simply to bring into focus those topics that you would most like to work on and master in your own professional life. Once you have identified your own growing edges, you can begin to design a plan of action that will get you from here to your goals as quickly and easily as possible.

ACTION PLANS

An action plan is very much like a New Year's resolution in that it is a commitment people make to achieve the particular goals they set for themselves. Most people have made New Year's resolutions in the past. Whenever I ask a group of people, "How many of us have made New Year's resolutions before?" most of the hands go up. When I then ask how many *have failed* at New Year's resolutions, most of the hands go up once again. Why is that? How is it that people so often set goals but don't achieve them? Does it have to be this way? Perhaps if people had a better understanding of what makes for success and failure, they could be more assured of succeeding with the goals that they set.

Let's turn now to some specific goals readers might set for themselves in connection with their work as IEP team members. We will then look at what makes for success and failure in any area where people make resolutions. Finally, a few sample action plans will be presented that readers can, if they wish, use as patterns for their own.

GOAL SETTING

In considering the steps team members can take to most effectively advance themselves as members of an IEP team, they have the opportunity, in a real sense, to develop IEPs of their own! After all, what is an IEP if not a set of specific, realistic, and personal goals supported by a clearly defined plan of action for achieving them? What follows now are some of the main categories a team member might consider. The list is not limited, however. If there are additional topics of interest and value that are not included here, by all means feel free to add them.

Suggested Reading

Surely one of the most familiar pathways for continuing growth is reading. Of course, there are not only long lists of worthwhile books and journals, but the list is forever expanding as new materials are developed and published. Any attempt that might be made here to list the best possible books and articles for professional development would soon be out of date. Rather than list any here, let me just make a general statement that there is no end of good material available, and one can always ask colleagues and supervisors for recommendations as to what might be worthwhile. Topics can include positive thinking, effective communication, emotional awareness and healing, the process of grieving, time management, motivation and leadership, team building, conflict resolution, mediation in special education. The list goes on and on. There is also a wealth of material available on the Internet. What is it that you are most eager to learn? What skills would you most like to enhance? Once a goal is established, finding relevant reading material should come easily with a few questions to coworkers, a visit to a library or bookstore, or a little Web surfing.

Training

The selection of personal and professional development training has much in common with what has just been said about reading. There is no end of workshops, seminars, and conferences in topics of professional growth. There are also vast hordes of speakers and trainers who are more than willing to come to you, and even to "build to suit." Many trainers have presentations on video- or audiocassette. Team members can start as before by deciding what topics would be most of interest and of help. It then becomes very easy to start asking around or searching on the Internet.

Keeping a Journal

Though very simple in concept, the keeping of a daily topical journal can be remarkably powerful. You might give it a try it for a week or so to see how it works for you by spending just a few minutes each day jotting notes in connection with your own growth objectives. If, for example, I am interested in working on my time management, I could jot notes at the end of each work day as to how well I organized, prioritized, and made use of my time today and what I would like to do differently tomorrow. If my target is improving diplomacy, I could jot notes at the end of the day about what I observed in others and in myself, so as to highlight what I could do differently as well as what I have done well. Another possibility (among so many) is just to keep a journal after each IEP team meeting and make notes about what the group did well, what could have been done better, what insights were made, what questions were raised, and so on. This simple investment of a few minutes each day can have dramatic benefits in just a short space of time.

Relaxation and Breathing Exercises

In the exploration of serenity in Chapter 6, it was emphasized that relaxation and breathing skills can be very helpful in preserving clear thinking and promoting flexible responses. Such skills are also of value in helping team members "keep cool and stay friendly" even when others are not. Like the keel of a sailboat, relaxation and breathing skills help members to keep their balance despite any turbulence around them. Tension and composure both have contagious effects in groups, and team members can choose which of these they want to contribute to the climate of their own team meetings. Many people have reported enormous benefits from working on their ability to simply relax and breathe. A few minutes of practice, perhaps twice each day for a week, can make an enormous difference. If you are like those who say, "I've been so tense for so long that when I relax, I get nervous," this one may be just what the doctor ordered!

Behavior Rehearsal

Otherwise known as role-playing or simply practice, behavior rehearsal is clearly one of the best things anyone can do to quickly develop new skills. Behavior rehearsal can be used with a number of the skills and techniques described in this book: making an introductory statement, setting ground rules, refocusing when participants wander or ramble, intervening when participants raise voices or break ground rules, probing for underlying interests, expressing supportive statements, or using any of the 25 specific intervention options. The list of possible applications for practice is enormous, and yet the method is very simple and always the same: set aside a few minutes once or twice each day to rehearse the skills you would like to master. You can role-play with a friend or an empty chair. You can pick up the phone and talk without dialing it. You can talk to the mirror, a pet, or a houseplant. Any of these can be valuable. I often role-play while driving alone in the car. I just roll up the windows and people think I'm singing. Try it. You'll like it! If I said that I wanted to play better tennis, you wouldn't blame me for practicing, would you? And if I wanted to play piano, you'd encourage me to practice, right? So, why not practice being a better communicator, a more supportive listener, a stronger leader, and a more effective team member?

Mental Rehearsal

What may come as a surprise to some people is that studies have shown that what people silently practice in their own imaginations can be just as productive as practicing in real life. Because of this simple but well-established fact, people can get many of the same benefits of practice by role-playing in their own imaginations—by clearly visualizing themselves handling a situation as they ideally wish to do.

Consider that worry is nothing more than negative mental rehearsal! Most people have a sense that worry is not productive and perhaps even harmful but without really understanding why this might be true. Let's look now at some reasons.

As illustrated by timelines of experience and self-talk alternatives (Chapter 4), emotional and physical responses follow from mental pictures, even more directly than they follow from the events a person experiences. Worry is invariably *negative* mental rehearsal—picturing negative outcomes—and this will and must result in negative feelings and stressing the physical body. The self-fulfilling prophecy (Chapter 6) encapsulates the fact that whatever it is we consistently and persistently imagine, we tend to attract, promote, or create. Those who expect failure tend to get it, and those who expect success tend to get that. So, what can worry (and its negative projections) ever do to help ensure positive outcomes? The point in emphasizing the downsides of worry is to encourage putting the same universal principles to work *for us* rather than against us—through positive mental rehearsal.

By choosing to hold only positive pictures, people create subconscious expectations that begin to play out in their everyday experience. Team members who expect success in the IEP environment are much more likely to see it, and those who decide to no longer entertain thoughts of conflict, stress, and difficulty will find them soon beginning to fade away. Team members can take this "power of positive thinking" a giant step further by setting aside a few minutes once or twice each day to relax, close their eyes, and intentionally hold clear, vivid images of handling situations exactly as they most wish to do—with confidence, respect, kindness, and skill. The more clearly they can see it, the more likely they will live it. Such is the power of mental rehearsal.

Team-Building Exercises

There are a number of daily or weekly activities a team member can do to strengthen the IEP team as a whole, and anyone can make a resolution to direct some time and attention in this direction. Some of these activities might include

- **Touching base with members before meetings** to remind them of time and location; to share an initial agenda; to clarify what will be needed by way of reports, observations, or other information; to ask for help being time conscious; and to ask if they have any questions, concerns, or recommendations that will help make the meeting more productive.

- **Following up with members after meetings:** As a matter of routine, or only as needed, a team member can make a point of phoning, e-mailing, or meeting with the others on the team to share thoughts, feelings, insights, and recommendations so as to keep awareness high and maximize effectiveness.

- **Greeting participants at the door:** When team members are coming from locations off campus, making a point to greet them at the school's entrance can go far toward helping them feel valued and welcome.

- **Making a point to interact with members outside of meetings:** Given that IEP meetings can be emotionally charged and sometimes difficult, some members have reported great benefits from establishing a relationship with participants at other school functions, such as parties, athletic events, PTA meetings, and similar gatherings that are not IEP-related and where participants are less on the spot.

Perhaps you can think of other possibilities for strengthening the IEP team outside of the meetings themselves. A few minutes addressing this issue in the context of the broader picture may be very helpful in showing interest, building trust, promoting involvement, and laying the foundation for strong IEP teams.

The Graduate Course

As a way of building a bridge between the "Collaboration in the IEP Environment" workshop and the work-a-day world, a series of daily exercises were developed with a different focus for each of 10 weeks. This series of exercises, called "The Graduate Course," includes and expands upon a number of topics covered in this book and is presented as an option in the appendix.

ENSURING YOUR SUCCESS

This chapter began by comparing an action plan to a New Year's resolution. They have much in common and very little difference, except perhaps in time of year, topics of focus, and the degree to which they have safeguards built in to ensure their success. It may be helpful to look now at why so many New Year's resolutions may have failed.

A close look at any genuine New Year's resolution will invariably reveal two key elements: an identified need and a sincere desire. That is, people decide to make resolutions in connection with things they think are important and things they really want to see happen. Quitting smoking, losing weight, being more patient, spending time with family, worrying less, enjoying life more—these are probably some of the more common resolutions that might appear on any year's "top 10" list. All include a sincere desire and identified need, both of which are certainly essential. Why then are people so often unsuccessful? Perhaps it is because these two key ingredients, while very important, are not by themselves sufficient.

Think for a moment of a business marketing plan. How many banks would lend money to a business that could not present an identified need and sincere desire? Probably very few. At the same time, how many banks would lend money to a business that could *only* present an identified need and sincere desire? Again, very, very few! What's missing of course is a road map—a specific and detailed plan of action as to how the business is going to get from vision to reality—how it will actually achieve its success and thereby assure the bank of a safe investment.

Returning now to New Year's resolutions, it simply isn't enough to set a goal (exercising more, thinking positively, slowing down, spending less, and so on). Like the business looking for investors, the one making a resolution must have a plan, and the more detailed and specific, the greater the likelihood of success. Fortunately, the plan doesn't need to be as complicated as a loan application, but it should have enough details to translate broad performance goals into bite-size pieces that can be easily accomplished. For reasons that may need no explanation, the recommendation is simply that an action plan should

1. Be relatively **short-term**

2. Be **realistic** and workable

3. Include **specific** tasks in a form that can be easily monitored

Applying this short list to a New Year's resolution, the well-intentioned but insufficient goal expressed as "to lose weight" will have a much better chance of success if expressed as

Lose at least 5 pounds per month for 3 months (March, April, May), using the XYZ diet, exercising three or more times per week, for at least 20 minutes each session, and sharing daily with my friend, Mary, to maintain accountability and receive support.

Consider what every child's IEP has in common. Don't they all include specific, realistic, and personalized goals, clearly defined pathways for achieving those goals, and specified periods of time until their next reassessment? The reason is simple: these make for success! Similarly, for professional development plans to have their greatest chance of success, they must include more than just an identified need and sincere desire. They must also incorporate the trio of key details (short-term, realistic, and specific) in outlining a plan that might look like any of the following.

Sample Personal Action Plans

1. For the month of October, after each IEP meeting, I will write in my journal for 5 minutes, making notes about what went well and what could have been improved.

2. I will use a written agenda and ask team members for their additions and endorsement at all my IEP meetings in April and then decide if this is something I want to continue.

3. I will work with the model checklist presented in Chapter 2 and role-play giving an introductory statement to an empty chair, twice a day for a week.

4. I will read one professional development book relating to IEP issues, each month for the next 3 months.

5. A week before each IEP meeting, I will touch base with the other members to be sure we are all prepared. I will make this a standard part of my work this term, and I will put reminder notes on my calendar for each week preceding an IEP meeting.

6. I will spend 5 minutes practicing relaxation and breathing exercises, twice each day for 2 weeks.

7. For 1 week, I will set aside 5 minutes on arrival at work and another 5 minutes at the end of the day to role-play the 25 intervention options (several times each) to an empty chair, in groups of three interventions at each session.

8. I will complete "The Graduate Course" during the fall term. I will form a group with two other IEP team members to do the exercises (independently) and to meet weekly to share insights and experiences so as to maintain accountability and receive support.

As will be readily apparent, some of the commitments listed above are very short-term (as little as a week) to more substantial (daily for 10 weeks). Some involve very little time (5 minutes after each meeting) and some involve considerably more (reading a book each month). The key is to develop a program that works for you—that involves the amount of time and focus that you feel comfortable to give. If it feels burdensome or is unrealistic, or if a genuine inner commitment is not present, the chance of success will be so much less. Remember, too, that the list of examples above is only for illustration. Feel free to make up any action plan that sounds good to you, but it is usually best to choose no more than three targets at a time so as to remain sufficiently focused. Another option is to let "The Graduate Course" be your only target.

Once an action plan has been followed to completion, a new action plan can be developed that involves different elements, or a person can continue to build on the skills already developed. As an example, for the month of April, I might focus on writing in my journal after meetings, on doing some professional reading, and on developing my relaxation skills. On May 1, I may decide that writing in my journal and reading are both action plan elements that I want to continue, but I don't feel a need to continue with relaxation exercises. Because I've done well with relaxation skills, I will now begin, instead, to work on role-plays of challenging situations. I will thus make role-playing the third element of my current and revised action plan.

Without a specific plan of action, the risk is great that good intentions will become like so many New Year's resolutions that did not bring the achievements that were considered important and even sincerely desired. I suspect that all readers of a book such as this one want their meetings to be efficient, productive, and pleasant. I believe that all IEP teams want to develop excellent IEPs for the children entrusted to them. Action plans will help teams achieve their shared objectives and give form to the vision of real decision-making partnership.

The Graduate Course

What follows is a series of exercises designed to strengthen your abilities as a valued member of your IEP team. Each exercise is designed to serve as an "experiment in living" for just 1 week (5 or 7 days, as you prefer). If you make a commitment to try these exercises for just 1 week each, you will do great things for your own benefit and for the benefit of those with whom you work. After 1 week, you will be in a wonderful position to decide if the exercise has been worthwhile and whether it is something you would like to continue or not. So, approach these as experiments and see where they lead. Hopefully, each exercise will be an easy task that will be fun as well as rewarding.

Week 1	Paste-Ups	Week 6	Active Reading
Week 2	Keeping a Journal	Week 7	Underlying Interests
Week 3	Parent Concerns	Week 8	Communication Skills
Week 4	Written Agendas	Week 9	Intervention Options
Week 5	Relaxation Exercises	Week 10	Supportive Statements

Paste-Ups

A *paste-up* is a visual aid designed to assist a person in holding a vision of success, thereby promoting whatever the person would like to create or develop in his or her life.

OBJECTIVE

To strengthen a vision of yourself as the person you would ideally like to be and to use that vision to help you move in the direction of your goals

MATERIALS

Poster board, old magazines, colored markers, scissors, and glue

TECHNIQUE *(to be completed as time permits over the course of a week)*

1. **Make a list** of characteristics of the ideal IEP team member, ones that you would like to adopt or strengthen for yourself. The list might include such qualities as having confidence, being a great listener, being empathic, showing understanding and concern, being assertive without being aggressive, being organized and prepared, having a great sense of humor, communicating respect even when seeing things differently, or any other qualities you would choose for yourself.

2. **Find your symbols.** Using old magazines, clip out words or pictures that represent the qualities you have listed. For example, if you would like more confidence, you might clip out a picture of an athlete receiving a medal. You might also clip out the words *confidence* or *new strength* to verbally represent your goal. You can also use your own artistic abilities to sketch, paint, or letter by hand the words and pictures that represent your personalized objectives.

3. **Make a poster** on which you creatively arrange the words and pictures you have collected, a poster that will serve as a visual representation of all of the qualities you would like to develop for yourself as a fantastic, valuable, and very capable IEP team member.

4. **Paste up your poster** of personalized images where you will see it often, and remind yourself every day of what you are rapidly becoming!

5. **Actively use your poster.** Spend a few minutes each day reviewing your poster, reaffirming *on a daily basis* your vision of success: "I *am* a person of confidence, kindness, and understanding!" [or whatever your personal goals]

What we imagine we can do, we can do.
What we persistently imagine we can do, we cannot help doing.

Keeping a Journal

The process of keeping a journal is simply one of making notes on a regular basis so as to hold in focus whatever a person may be trying to learn, create, or develop.

OBJECTIVE

To strengthen your skills as an effective IEP team member by keeping a daily journal of key observations, insights, and experiences

TECHNIQUE

1. **Make a commitment** that you will make notes on a daily basis of insights and observations that relate to your IEP team experiences.

2. **Keep a journal** each day in whatever form works best for you. It could be at the end of each IEP meeting, but if you only have two or less per week, expand your focus to all meetings or all interactions with others at work. Your notes should record such things as

   • What you did well and want to continue

   • What challenges you encountered

   • What you might have done better

- What insights you had
- What resolutions you would make for the future

3. **Continue through 1 week** and then evaluate whether this has been helpful and whether it is something you would like to continue. If so, in what form would you like to continue it?

SAMPLE JOURNAL ENTRIES

OCTOBER 12, 1:45 P.M. While waiting for the parents to arrive for our IEP team meeting, I am aware of feeling tense and a sense of dread. These people are always so difficult—belligerent and unpleasant, like everyone is against them when we are only trying to help. Okay, so I realize I am thinking negatively. How could I see this differently? Breathe, relax. See them as people who have had troubles before and are afraid of us and just trying to get a fair shake for their son. Okay, resolution: *I refuse to see them as the enemy.* We are partners in a joint challenge—to develop the best IEP for their son.

OCTOBER 12, 5 P.M. I didn't bite on any hooks and just stayed friendly and pleasant, and they began to relax and be more agreeable. They even laughed a few times—and thanked us at the end. (That never happened before!)

Parent Concerns

OBJECTIVE

To brainstorm with other IEP team members and develop meaningful responses to common parent concerns

TECHNIQUE

1. **Review:** Spend 10 minutes each day this week reviewing the list of 12 parent concerns presented in the Introduction.

2. **Make specific suggestions** that might be workable in your school or district.

3. **Follow up** on your suggestions in whatever ways work best for you, and make notes about the support, resistance, challenges, results, and insights you encounter.

OPTION

Make an agreement with two or three others to do this exercise together—to review the list of concerns, decide what responses seem most workable, and share ideas about what can be done in your own school or district.

Set up a series of conferences, in person or by phone, each day this week, and share your ideas and experiences together as you make an effort to act on your group's recommendations. These conferences may extend beyond the 1 week of the exercise.

ABBREVIATED EXAMPLE

Frequently voiced parent concern #2: Each participant at IEP meetings may have differing objectives and constraints—financial, staffing, available resources, time, and so on—yet too often with poor understanding of, and poor communication with, the other participants.

SUGGESTIONS: 1) Communicate and make a plan before each team meeting so that people are really present and not just there in body. 2) Show active listening skills. 3) Maintain a focus on what's best for the child.

MY NOTES: *Will touch base with all IEP team members a few days before every meeting to be sure they have their schedules clear, are aware of the agenda, and come prepared. Will phone the parents and ask if they have any questions, reassure them that I am pleased they are coming, and encourage them to speak openly. Will stay aware of my listening skills. Will make a point of reminding all participants, as part of my introductory comments, that our purpose is always for the benefit of [child's name].*

Written Agendas

Some of the most common complaints about meetings of any kind arise when the participants are not clear about why they are meeting. A written agenda helps the group stay on task, budget their time, and address all relevant issues.

OBJECTIVE

To use a written agenda at all IEP meetings for a week and see whether it is helpful

Note: If you have very few IEP meetings in a week, use an agenda at all staff or other meetings, even informal ones, as a way of seeing how agendas work. For example, when meeting someone for a parent conference or a working lunch, make a point of asking how much time you have together and what things you want to be sure to talk about.

TECHNIQUE

1. **Invite buy-in.** If this will be the first time the group uses a written agenda, ask the members in advance if they would be willing to try it and see if it is helpful in making good use of the limited time the group has. [Asking is affirming.] If they say "yes," then go to Step 2.

2. **Set a preliminary agenda.** On a white board or flip chart (or in a written handout), block in the topics for the day's meeting, as well as the person who will be responsible for each topic.

3. **Finalize the agenda and follow it.** When the group arrives, ask for confirmation and any additions from the group: "Does this sound like a good plan for today? Anyone else have any other issues we should make time for today?"

OPTIONS

Once the list of topics is complete, ask the people responsible for those agenda items how much time they think will be sufficient for that part of the agenda. Then ask a group member to volunteer to be the timekeeper—to alert the participants if they are getting off task or going beyond their time announcements. [Note that setting times and appointing a timekeeper may only be necessary as a learning exercise or for groups that often struggle with focus and time management.]

EXAMPLE

SAMPLE AGENDA

Introductions and stage-setting	Sue	5 minutes
Classroom observations	Paul	5 minutes
Test results	Maria	10 minutes
Home observations and report	Jane	5 minutes
Is specially designed instruction still required?	team	1 minute
How have extended services been working and are they still required?	André	5 minutes
Modifications to Sally's IEP	team	20 minutes
Possibility of transportation assistance	Jane	5 minutes

Relaxation Exercises

Relaxation is important in the IEP environment for the simple reason that if the team members are not reasonably relaxed, they are probably unnecessarily tense. Tension has several negative side effects. For one thing, tension tends to be contagious in that it promotes similar tension in others (just as relaxation tends to promote relaxation in others). Furthermore, a high level of tension interferes with clear thinking and with caring for and support of others (as opposed to protection of self). Also, tension accompanies stress, and stress cannot take hold when true relaxation is present.

OBJECTIVE

To strengthen your relaxation skills and observe what differences they make in your IEP teamwork

TECHNIQUE

Choose two 5-minute segments each day, perhaps when you first arrive at work and again at the end of the workday. Make arrangements so that you will not be disturbed, perhaps by closing the door and hanging a "do not disturb" sign.

1. **Practice:** Sit upright with your back not supported and then simply

- **Breathe:** Observe the flowing in and flowing out of your breath. Do not change it in any way. Just observe it and be aware of the depth and rate of your breathing.

- **Relax:** Observe the muscles of your head and face. Be aware of any tension you may feel there. As you become aware of any tension you are holding, simply release it and let it go. Allow yourself to become more and more fully relaxed. Similarly, observe and relax your neck and shoulders. Next, observe and relax your arms, hands, and fingers. Progress slowly and methodically throughout your entire body, all the way down to your legs, feet, and toes, each time observing, becoming aware, then relaxing and letting go.

- **Imagine:** See yourself in a beautiful and very comfortable setting, perhaps lying on a beach in the Bahamas or sitting beside a waterfall on a scenic woodland trail. Hold this image, clearly and vividly, through a few moments of silence.

2. **Score:** Jot a few notes about your experience, and give yourself a score on a scale of 1–10 for how fully relaxed you were able to become.

3. **Apply:** Observe how your level of tension rises or falls during the course of your work activities. Note what difference it makes for yourself and those around you when, instead of becoming tense, you are able to remain relaxed and comfortable. Make notes of any observations that strike you as significant.

Active Reading

Although professional reading is something most team members are already doing on a regular basis, there is a way to deepen the value of the reading and strengthen the carryover into practical experience.

OBJECTIVE

To use concurrent journaling as a way to highlight the practical applications of a particular reading

TECHNIQUE

1. **Make a commitment** that this week you will read a certain book or professional journal. Let this exercise be for quality not quantity, so pick an amount of reading that will not be too demanding for you to comfortably complete—however many pages, chapters, or articles you believe would be a reasonable goal for you.

2. **Be alert** to the practical implications of any insight, technique, theory, or study that is described in your reading.

3. **Make a written list** of the points of value that you discover as you read.

EXAMPLE

This is an excerpt from a real newspaper article about parents' mistrust of schools:

> "There are parents out there who won't be that blunt, but I don't trust you . . . . Think of how much more productive the entire process would be if you trusted me and I trusted you." Some parents describe school meetings in which they don't feel welcome, their input isn't valued and those who ask questions are labeled troublemakers.

Sample Notes

To apply the technique of this week's exercise to the above article, you would simply jot a few notes as you read, and they might look something like this:

1. Do the parents I work with trust me? How can I find out? I could watch for their cues or maybe ask them directly.

2. When I work with people I don't trust, what does that feel like? How do I show or hide it? I probably don't say anything, but I feel suspicious of what they say and I may be looking for their ulterior motives.

3. What if it's true that trust is lacking? How could we fix it? I can "share my good intention" that we develop a climate of trust. I can ask them to let me know if they suspect I am being untrustworthy.

4. Do the parents I work with feel welcome? How can I help them feel more welcome? Will watch this.

Underlying Interests

OBJECTIVE

To develop skills in asking questions that help to clarify the reasons behind the positions that people have taken. Doing so shows caring and respect, valuing, and inclusion. It also helps bring to light much-needed information that can be very helpful for reaching consensus.

TECHNIQUE

1. **Observe:** During interactions with others this week, be alert to opportunities to ask questions that probe for the thoughts, feelings, and objectives behind whatever it is that people are asking for.

2. **Make daily notes** about your experiences and observations by
    - Including an overview of what happened
    - Underlining your probing questions
    - Noting how others responded to your probing questions

EXAMPLES OF PROBING QUESTIONS AND STATEMENTS

1. You must have good reasons for that. Tell us some of them.

2. Help me understand your thoughts about that.

3. Say some more about that; how might that address the issue?

4. What do you see happening if we go that route?

5. How might that idea be helpful?

6. What benefits do you think we can expect if we try that?

7. What harm would come if we tried it his way?

SAMPLE JOURNAL ENTRY
with overview, underlines, and outcomes

Monday

Overview: Received a phone call from Mary asking if we could do some new reading assessments on Johnny before the IEP team meeting. Instead of "We really don't have time to do that" or similar explanations, I asked her, "Would you say some more about that?" She explained that she believed his reading scores are lower than they should be because of his test anxiety and not his real abilities. I asked her, "In what way might more testing be helpful?" and she said, "I just think it would refute the idea that he's not reading at the level of his peers."

Outcome: We talked for a few minutes, and she agreed we could raise this issue with the team when we get together next week and see what the others think, and that maybe more testing wasn't the answer if Johnny's anxiety was really the issue. I noticed that she was initially a little huffy but soon became more relaxed. She seemed to appreciate a chance to share her thoughts and thanked me for my time.

Communication Skills

OBJECTIVE

To improve your awareness and abilities in each of the four key areas of effective communications:

1. Hold a focus (one person and one issue at a time)

2. Talk from the heart (clearly express feelings and wants)

3. Listen with respect (listen like a sponge)

4. Maintain the spirit of friendship

TECHNIQUE

1   **Keep a log** each day this week.

2. **Give yourself a score** on a scale of 1 to 10 (with 10 being perfect) for how well you did in each of these key areas.

3. **Add notes** about any key observations or insights.

EXAMPLE

Day	Focus	Heart	Listen	Spirit	Notes
Monday	6	7	4	8	*Busy and rushed today. Hard to listen when I have so much to do.*
Tuesday	3	4	4	8	*Pure chaos today. Really messed up on this home-work.*
Wednesday	7	7	9	10	*Did better today—tried to show I was really with the other person.*
Thursday	9	5	7	10	*Not really shar-ing my feelings. Mary said I really seemed calmer.*
Friday	9	7	8	8	*One of my better days. Listening better but still having trouble with feelings.*

Intervention Options

If any school football team wanted to become better at football, the members would have to get out on the field and practice, right? And if a chess team wanted to become better at chess, the players would have to make time to practice their skills, too. Similarly, if IEP team members want to become better at conflict prevention and resolution, they will benefit a great deal from practice in this regard, as well.

OBJECTIVE

To develop your ability to comfortably use a variety of conflict prevention and resolution approaches by practicing for a few minutes twice each day for a week

TECHNIQUE

1. **Make time.** Choose two 5-minute segments each day, perhaps when you first arrive at work and again at the end of the workday. Make arrangements so that you will not be disturbed, perhaps by closing the door and hanging a "do not disturb" sign.

2. **Plan.** Divide the 25 prevention/intervention options presented at the end of Chapter 7 into groups, in order, so as to make eight

groups of three plus one. In a 5-day week, at two sessions per day, you would have ten 5-minute sessions, so it will be easy to cover all groups of three at least once.

3. **Practice.** To an empty chair or into the phone (without dialing) or to one of your potted plants, say aloud each of this session's three prevention/intervention options. Repeat each one several times and strive to express sincerity and respect.

OPTIONS

If you want to make this exercise even more powerful, imagine you are talking to a particular IEP team member and use that person's name in your practice session.

As another option, ask a co-worker to role-play with you. You can take turns and give each other feedback about tones of voice, eye contact, hand gestures, facial expressions, postures, and fidgeting. You can also discuss how relaxed, comfortable, friendly, sincere, and caring you seemed.

Supportive Statements

A universal feature of conflict is unpleasant emotions, such as feeling hurt, offended, belittled, discounted, scared, intimidated, and so on. A common interest of people in groups is to have their feelings respected and understood, and this can serve many helpful purposes. Very often, all it takes is recognition of feelings for them to move and change. (As an example, when I acknowledge how upset you must feel, you may begin to feel less upset.)

OBJECTIVE

To develop your ability to show support for the feelings of others, so as to communicate caring, raise mutual awareness and understanding, facilitate problem solving, and assist in the resolution of any unpleasant feelings

TECHNIQUE

1. **Make a written list** of supportive statements similar to those below:

   - Help me understand your feelings about that.
   - How are you doing with that?
   - What was that like for you?
   - This seems to be really hard for you, right?

2. **Expand your list.** As you hear others express supportive statements or as you think of new ones of your own, add them to your list. If possible, exchange lists with others who are also working on this exercise (by phone, by e-mail, or in person).

3. **Make written notes** of your observations this week as you express supportive statements to others: what did you say, how did they respond, what did you learn, how might you do it differently? Remember that sincerity is important—"it's not just the words but the music."

SAMPLE NOTES

Wednesday: Sarah seemed upset about something one of her students said to her, so I said, "Sounds like that really hurt your feelings." And she snapped at me, "No, it didn't. I just thought it was rude." So then I thought, "Wow, this stuff can really get you in trouble," but then later I thought that maybe she's just not comfortable letting her feelings show. I talked to my husband about it. He thought that maybe if I'd said, "Sounds like that was hard to hear," it might have sat better with her.

Index

Page references followed by *t* indicate tables.